HOW EVERYTHING WORKS

Electricity, Technology, Engineering, Robotics, The Human Body, Ecosystems, Flight, Sound, and So Much More!

JAMIE MYERS

ISBN: 978-1-957590-44-8

For questions, email: Support@AwesomeReads.org

Please consider writing a review!

Just visit: AwesomeReads.org/review

FREE BONUS

SCAN TO GET OUR NEXT
BOOK FOR FREE!

TABLE OF CONTENTS

INTRODUCTION

If you've ever wondered how a device works, you're not alone. With so many advances in technology, it's understandable to be curious. But instead of taking apart your parents' computer or trying to build your own electrical device, you can find many of your answers here.

WELCOME TO THE WORLD OF WONDERS

In our fascinating world of wonders, you'll explore strange, new things and be awed by what you'll learn.

In this book, we'll take you on an exciting journey deep into the world of science and technology. From the human body to robots, we'll learn what makes things tick. Buckle your seatbelt; you're in for a wild ride.

By the time you're finished reading, you'll know lots of things to share with your friends and use in school. And the best part? Your curiosity about how things work will be satisfied.

WHY LEARN HOW THINGS WORK?

Science is founded on discovering how things work. Every scientific invention started with someone trying to figure out how something works.

Humans have been on a quest for knowledge since cavemen discovered fire, and as technology has become more complex, the demand for knowledge has only increased.

To fix broken things, you must know how they work first. You also need to know how the latest and greatest technology works if you want to set it up properly. Preserving the planet is essential if we want to continue using its resources. It's important to know how things work to do this, including recycling and conservation strategies.

HOW TO USE THIS BOOK

Throughout this book's 19 chapters, we'll explore topics by explaining what it is and how it works. You'll get to know each topic well by the time you're done reading. Each topic is broken down into three sections to help make it easier to understand and to give you as much information as possible.

CHAPTER ONE:
THE HUMAN BODY

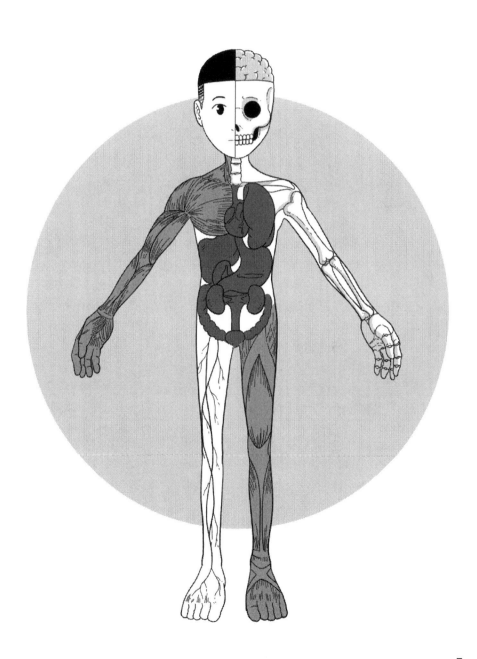

The human body is one of the most amazing things to learn about because its systems ensure your survival. Let's take a look at how the human body works, from the atoms that structure life to the organs and systems that maintain the body's overall function.

ANATOMY AND PHYSIOLOGY

Two important words that come up when you're discussing the human body are anatomy and physiology. Anatomy focuses on the various structures of the human body and how they are organized. Physiology is the study of how human body parts function, focusing on what they do and how they do it.

Anatomy has two separate areas of study: gross anatomy, which is the study of body parts that can be seen without a microscope (such as the stomach, heart, and liver) and histology, which is the study of body parts that must be viewed through a microscope (such as the lining of the small intestine).

Knowing the parts of the body and how they function is important. Because of this, many students study anatomy and physiology simultaneously.

Living systems have distinctive structures and are made up of several important pieces. On the smallest level are the atoms. Multiple atoms form bonds with one another to create molecules. The chemical bonds between the atoms and these molecules create the foundation for all life.

Billions of cells make up the human body, the smallest unit of life on the planet. Within cells are specialized bodies called organelles that perform cellular functions. Some cells are specialized, which means they are dedicated to a specific part of the body, like the liver.

When similar cells with similar characteristics are grouped together to perform a common function, they create tissue. Several types of tissues then work together to form your organs. For example, your heart isn't just one type of tissue. It's actually made up of four types: epithelial, muscle, connective, and nervous tissues. Several organs can also work together to achieve a specific goal, creating an organ system. At least two organs are required to form a system.

An organism is the total sum of all these parts. It is the entire system within living things. This means an organism can obtain and use energy as well as respond to any changes in its environment.

CIRCULATORY AND RESPIRATORY SYSTEMS

The circulatory and respiratory systems are vital for the human body to function. Without either of these systems, you would not be able to survive. So, let's take a look at what each one is made up of and how they work.

Circulatory System

Your body's circulatory system is made of three main parts: heart, blood vessels, and blood. This system's job is to deliver oxygen, and a form of sugar called glucose to the cells throughout your body. Once that part of its job is complete, it then works to remove waste.

The heart is essentially a pump and is made up of four chambers. As the heart relaxes, it fills with blood. Then, it contracts to push that blood to every area of the body. The chambers have valves between them that keep the blood from moving the wrong way through the system.

There's something special about the heart's muscle cells: They are electrically connected with no need for a nerve signal to cause their contraction. Because of this one-of-a-kind connection, your heart can maintain its rhythmic beating to effectively pump blood throughout the system.

Your blood vessels move blood throughout the body, regulating the flow to the different parts as needed. They receive signals from the nervous system that direct them to expand or contract. Blood vessels come in many different sizes, with the biggest ones being closest to the heart.

Blood has several important parts, including platelets, red blood cells, and white blood cells. It also contains a mix of different chemicals, hormones, and proteins. Platelets are like the repair cells of the system, repairing any damage that occurs. Red blood cells are loaded with hemoglobin, a protein that allows the cells to move oxygen throughout the body. White blood cells are constantly fighting invading germs, bacteria, and viruses like tiny soldiers inside your body.

Respiratory System

Your respiratory system is responsible for your breathing. It has several parts, including your blood vessels, lungs, and airways. In a way, it is like the circulatory system because it involves the movement of oxygen. This system is also the reason why you can smell different scents. Additionally, it is broken into two parts: the upper respiratory tract and the lower respiratory tract.

Your upper respiratory tract cleans and warms the air you breathe before allowing it to pass to the lower airways. This part of the respiratory system also has a big role in your ability to speak, and it moves food and fluids to the digestive tract.

On the other hand, your lower respiratory tract moves the incoming warm, clean air into a structure that looks like an upside-down tree. This tree is made of your trachea, bronchi, and bronchioles. Once the air passes through this structure, it will reach the alveoli, where it can contact your blood.

The larynx divides the digestive and respiratory systems. This structure features a special flap called the epiglottis, which closes over the airway to prevent food and liquids from entering. You might have heard of this body part for another reason. It is primarily involved in speech production.

Another important part of the respiratory system is the diaphragm, the muscle that allows you to inhale and exhale.

Your airways have unique features and functions that allow them to protect you from viruses and bacteria. Certain cells throughout your airways secrete mucus to create a protective layer that stops bacteria from growing and traps anything bad that you may have inhaled. These cells work with hair-like cells (cilial cells) to move the trapped things and mucus from the airways.

The lungs are responsible for allowing the exchange of oxygen between the inhaled air and your blood. The alveoli are located deep within the lungs and have very thin walls that help make this exchange work easily.

DIGESTIVE AND NERVOUS SYSTEMS

Your digestive and nervous systems are two more major organ systems within your body. Your digestive system breaks down food to extract the necessary energy and nutrients. The nervous system can be considered the driver of your body, as it controls all the other systems. Let's see what they do and how they do it.

Digestive System

The digestive system is made up of two parts, including the gastrointestinal tract (GI) and the biliary system. When you eat, the food travels from your mouth into your esophagus. Then, it moves into the stomach, where it is digested. From there, your GI tract moves the food to the small intestine before it passes to the large intestine. Finally, the waste products from your food will pass through the anus. The biliary system is made up of the organs that assist digestion, including the pancreas, gall bladder, liver, and bile ducts.

Your liver and pancreas are considered dual-purpose organs because they do two things. The liver secretes bile to aid in digestion and helps detoxify the blood. On the other hand, the pancreas produces enzymes that break down hormones and proteins. Because of this, the pancreas is responsible for managing blood sugar.

Nervous System

The nervous system controls your whole body and is complex. There are two primary branches: the central nervous system (CNS) and the peripheral nervous system (PNS). The CNS has just two parts: the spine and the brain. The PNS is spread all over the body, starting from the spine. The PNS has different branches, including the somatic nervous system (SNS) and the autonomic nervous system (ANS).

The ANS also has two branches. You may have heard of the "fight or flight" response to danger. The sympathetic nervous system manages this reaction. On the other hand, the parasympathetic nervous system is responsible for resting and conserving energy. This is also called the "rest or digest" system.

The nervous system works by sending messages through special cells called neurons. Your body has three types of neurons, each with a different job. Motor neurons are responsible for movement, speech, and the ability to breathe and swallow. Sensory neurons tell your brain the information you take in from your senses, like what you see or hear. The third type is interneurons, which allow the motor neurons to communicate with the sensory neurons.

As you can see, the human body is truly fascinating. Now that you have a good idea of its different systems and how they work, let's look at other living things: plants and ecosystems.

CHAPTER TWO:
PLANTS AND ECOSYSTEMS

The natural world is made up of living and nonliving parts, one of which is plant life. Plants are unique life forms, as they not only produce their own food, but they end up being food for many animals. Let's journey through your average plant's life cycle and learn how ecosystems work.

PHOTOSYNTHESIS AND PLANT LIFE CYCLE

Photosynthesis and the plant life cycle are two of the most important processes in the natural world. Photosynthesis is so important that all life depends on it. So, let's explore these processes and how they work.

Photosynthesis

Photosynthesis is the process green plants use to produce their own food. It relies on sunlight and is critical to human life. Without photosynthesis, green plants would not exist; without green plants, animals would not exist.

Green plants have leaves containing a substance called chlorophyll. Photosynthesis requires chlorophyll, sunlight, carbon dioxide, gas, and water. The plants absorb carbon dioxide from the air, while water is absorbed from the soil.

Chlorophyll interacts with sunlight to absorb energy. The plant then uses that energy to transform water and carbon dioxide into sugars, a natural energy source, and oxygen, a waste product. Some sugars are used as food, and the rest are stored for later use. The plant releases any produced oxygen back into the air.

Plant Life Cycle

Plants have male and female reproductive organs, which they use in pollination. This process involves the anther releasing pollen that is transferred to the stigma. There, one of two things can happen. If the pollen transfers between the anther and stigma on the same plant, then self-pollination has occurred. Cross-pollination occurs if the pollen is transferred between one plant's anther and another's stigma.

Flowers are usually pollinated by insects or the wind. Insect-pollinated flowers have sweet scents and bright colors that attract insects looking for food. Pollen is sticky and attaches to the insects. It is then carried to another plant, where it is brushed onto the stigma. Wind-pollinated flowers tend to be lighter in color and have no scent. Their anthers are outside the flower, allowing the wind easy access to the pollen.

The pollen must land on a stigma of the same plant species for fertilization to occur. Fertilization begins when the pollen grain grows a pollen tube. This tube travels down through the style, ultimately reaching the ovary. The male reproductive cells or gametes move through the pollen tube to join with the female reproductive cells in the ovules. After being fertilized, the ovule turns into a seed that contains a food store and an embryo. The ovary wall typically forms a fruit or pod around it to protect the seeds.

When the seeds are ready to be planted, they have to be spread far and wide from their parent plants and each other. This ensures they have the space needed to grow and obtain nutrients. Seeds are carried around in multiple ways. One of the main methods is by animals. They eat the fruit but cannot digest the seeds, which are then passed from the body whole in their poop. Other fruits have hook-like features that allow them to catch on passing materials, like clothing or fur. They hitch a ride and then get dropped off somewhere new. Other plants have adapted to transporting their seeds by wind or water.

The seeds then make their home in the ground where they are deposited. When the seeds successfully germinate, their protective outer shell opens, allowing the embryo to grow. For this process to work, the soil must be healthy, the seeds must have access to water, and the temperature must be warm enough.

As the plant grows, it develops roots down into the ground, and a shoot grows from the ground. The shoot will grow into a stem and support the growth of the leaves, which are responsible for photosynthesis. The plant continues growing until it reaches full maturity when the entire cycle begins again.

ECOSYSTEM DYNAMICS AND INTERACTIONS

An ecosystem is made up of living or biotic elements and nonliving or abiotic elements that interact with the weather and landscape to create a bubble of life. Every part of an ecosystem depends in some way on every other part. For example, if the temperature changes, some plants may no longer be able to grow in the ecosystem. This could affect animal life, as they depend on those plants for food. So, the plants in this example are directly influenced by the temperature, and the animals are indirectly influenced by it.

Ecosystems come in many sizes, including small tide pools on the beach. Multiple ecosystems are connected through biomes, bigger organizations made of large areas of atmosphere, land, or sea.

Within an ecosystem, there is a hierarchy. At the bottom are the producers who make their own food. Next are the animals that eat those producers. On the next level are the animals who eat producers and consumers. Then, there are the animals that just eat the consumers. At the very top are the apex predators that are the main consumers in the food chain.

ENVIRONMENTAL CONSERVATION

Many ecosystems are in danger due to human carelessness. We protect the natural world when we take steps to conserve natural resources sustainably and ethically.

There are two types of resources: renewable and nonrenewable. Renewable resources are replaceable and include living things because they can reproduce. However, renewable resources have limitations. Too much hunting or harvesting can impact an entire species. Nonrenewable resources are not replaceable and include things like fossil fuels. Once these are gone, they are gone forever.

When rules are established to use natural resources sustainably, companies are prevented from removing everything. For example, if there weren't rules about how much wood can be harvested from the rainforests, companies could just cut down all the trees, leaving a wasteland in their wake. This would result in massive destruction of the area's biodiversity.

Conservation faces many challenges, the biggest of which is people's unwillingness to give up their conveniences. Consider how people rely on their cars, but cars contribute to air pollution. By walking more or taking public transportation, everyone could reduce the effects of air pollution produced by driving. However, the convenience of hopping in the driver's seat when you need to run down the road for something generally outweighs the ecological benefit of walking.

Many businesses are driven by profit, preventing their commitment to conservation. For example, if a timber company was informed that cutting down fewer trees could protect the animal population in the forest, what would their response be? While they could help the environment by doing this, they would earn less profit. In most cases, they choose profits over conservation.

If you're interested in contributing to the conservation efforts, there are plenty of things you can do. Recycling is a great start. This practice keeps unnecessary waste out of landfills and allows materials to be reused.

Now that we've completed our trip through these interesting areas of science, let's move on to animals and wildlife.

CHAPTER THREE: ANIMALS AND WILDLIFE

Rounding out our exploration of living creatures, we come to animals and wildlife. These two groups of organisms are incredible in that they can adapt and evolve over time. Let's look at what this means.

ADAPTATIONS AND BEHAVIORS

Animals' adaptations and behaviors ensure they survive as their environments change. They typically adapt over generations, and their behaviors help them respond to their environment.

Adaptations

Animals adapt to survive, but it's a process that happens slowly. When one generation of a species finds an advantageous trait, members of the species will produce offspring with the trait. As generations pass, the number of members with that trait will steadily increase until it becomes a general feature of the entire species.

Adaptations can be structural or behavioral. If the adaptation is structural, it is an actual part of the organism. If it is behavioral, it affects the organism's response to environmental stimulation. One example of a structural adaptation is the ability of a cactus plant to retain water inside to prevent dehydration in the desert. Seasonal migration is a great example of a behavioral type of adaptation. Birds will fly away from winter conditions and return to their homes when the area returns to a comfortable temperature.

In many cases, adaptations result from a change in the organism's habitat. These allow the organism to survive dramatic changes or take advantage of a certain environmental feature. There are also cases where an adaptation or set of adaptations can be so distinctive that it causes one species to split into two, a process called speciation.

Behaviors

The word behavior refers to how animals act. With thousands of animals across the planet, many have unique methods for hunting, communicating, hiding from predators, and more.

Instinctive behaviors are those with which animals are born and happen in response to certain signals that may come from inside the body or the outside environment. Instinctive behavior does not require thinking. Instead, the response occurs automatically based on the type of signal received.

Learned behaviors are those that animals are not born with. These behaviors change according to environmental signals. Animals take in information about their surroundings through their senses and then use that information to create new behaviors to help them survive.

BIODIVERSITY AND CONSERVATION

Every environment in the world is made up of a variety of plant and animal life. This is known as biodiversity. This term applies to small areas like deserts, the entire planet, or any of the habitats in between.

Biodiversity helps humans thrive. For example, many medications we use to treat illnesses come from plants. If biodiversity were reduced, certain plants might be wiped out before we identify their medical applications.

However, human behavior generally hurts biodiversity. Think about the last time you saw a big store being built. What was there before construction started? Most likely, it was an area with trees. All those trees need to be cleared to create space for a building. But those trees provided a home to many plants and animals. When plants are destroyed, animals are forced to relocate.

Conservation practices help ensure that an area remains biodiverse. The same is true of the preservation of species. One way species are preserved is by reintroducing it in a specific location. For example, at one time, there were no wolves left in Yellowstone National Park. The loss of the wolves caused a significant imbalance in the ecosystem. Officials recognized the need for wolves to control elk and deer populations. A plan was put in place to reintroduce them slowly. Since the original 14 wolves were released in 1995, their numbers have grown to more than 120. By restoring balance to the system, the number of beavers and certain species of trees has also increased.

Rehabilitation centers and zoos are also concerned with animal conservation. These facilities allow animals to breed under protected conditions, increasing their numbers until they are ready to be released back into their natural habitats. These conservation methods are especially important when an animal is close to extinction. Several centers and zoos throughout the world are focused on maintaining the last of a species.

EVOLUTIONARY PROCESSES

Evolution is a theory based on the idea that every living organism evolved from an earlier version of itself. This theory is widely accepted by scientists and is supported by scientific evidence.

Fossils are one of the main sources of information about evolution. Fossils clearly show that creatures that once lived are much different than those that live today.

Inside every living thing is DNA, which carries genes. Genes are responsible for passing traits across generations. By studying DNA, scientists have found that many species likely developed from common ancestors.

The key process of evolution occurs when an organism has different genes than the other members of the species. Variances in genes are generally a result of mutation. Most variances will either harm the organism or improve its chances of survival.

Charles Darwin is the true force behind modern evolution theory. He outlined his theory in his book, On the Origin of Species, published in 1859. He would write another work specifically dedicated to the evolution of humans in which he determined that humans evolved from apes.

Today, DNA is one of the main ways to research evolution. It allows scientists to determine how closely related certain species are based on their evolutionary ancestors.

Animals, biodiversity, and evolution are super interesting, aren't they? In the next chapter, we'll stick with the natural world for a bit longer. Instead of living things, we'll focus on the seasons and climates.

CHAPTER FOUR:
SEASONS AND CLIMATE SYSTEMS

In the last two chapters, we've discussed the living components of ecosystems. Now, it's time to turn our focus to the nonliving parts: seasons and climate systems. An area's climate greatly impacts what can survive there, from the smallest plants to the largest animals. The different seasons affect how plants and animals interact with their environment. Here's a closer look at what this means.

EARTH'S ROTATION AND ORBIT

The planet continuously rotates on its axis, which creates day and night. At the same time, it orbits around the sun. While it rotates and orbits, it is slightly tilted on its axis. The axis is like an invisible line that runs from one pole to the other, directly through the planet's center. The tilt, though slight, is enough to cause part of the Earth to be closer to the sun than the rest of the planet. In other words, different planet sections receive different levels of heat and sunlight.

Why does this matter? This tilt creates a pattern that ultimately creates seasons. Without the tilt, seasons would not exist.

Have you ever noticed that shadows don't stay the same throughout the day? This is due to Earth's rotation and orbit. As the planet rotates, shadows are created in relation to the sun. As the planet rotates and the sun appears to move through the sky, shadows will change shape and direction based on its position in relation to the sun. If the planet didn't rotate or orbit the sun, shadows would stay the same.

Another important thing to know about the Earth's rotation and orbits is that it takes one day to complete a single rotation. During this period, the planet's surface is warmed by the sun. Without this rotation, one side of the planet would always be cold and dark while the other would always be sunlit and hot.

An orbit is also known as a revolution. It takes one year for the Earth to complete its revolution around the sun. Earth rotates at roughly 1,000 miles per hour (1,600 kilometers per hour) and orbits the sun at about 67,000 miles per hour (107,800 kilometers per hour).

ATMOSPHERIC CIRCULATION AND WEATHER PATTERNS

Atmospheric circulation and weather patterns significantly impact weather and climate. Understanding these two important parts of climate systems is essential to get the whole picture.

Atmospheric Circulation

Atmospheric circulation, which is the movement of air on a large scale, distributes heat across Earth. Masses of air are moved around the globe in wind belts. When observed over decades, the wind belts appear stable with minor changes. However, seasonal and annual changes can occur. Large-scale convection patterns and the Coriolis effect also influence the wind belts.

The Coriolis effect refers to how circulating air is deflected in the northern and southern hemispheres because of the tilt of the Earth's axis. In the northern hemisphere, objects will be deflected to the right, while they will be deflected to the left in the southern hemisphere.

Because of the tilt and rotation of the Earth, the amount of solar radiation an area receives is constantly shifting.

There are three atmospheric systems known as circulation cells: the Hadley cell, the Ferrel cell, and the polar cell. These cells move moisture, heat, and air throughout the atmosphere.

The Hadley cell, named for George Hadley, an English physicist and meteorologist, is based on the idea that air journeys toward the equator at the lower latitudes. When it reaches its destination, the air is warmed and rises. Once it reaches the upper atmosphere, it moves toward the pole in the hemisphere where it is located. This results in the formation of a Hadley convection cell.

The Ferrel cell, identified by William Ferrel, accounts for surface air moving toward the poles and east. The air in the higher levels of the atmosphere moves toward the west and equator.

Polar cells are formed when air ascends and moves toward the poles in higher latitudes. Once it reaches the poles, it sinks and creates areas of high atmospheric pressure called polar highs. On the surface, air moves outward from the polar highs. This action causes the formation of the polar easterlies, which are east-blowing surface winds.

Weather Patterns

Weather (the atmospheric conditions of a given location at a specified time) is made up of large global patterns in the atmosphere. These patterns are caused by interactions between the planet's motion in space and interaction with solar radiation.

Weather is affected by short-term changes in atmospheric conditions, including pressure systems. Pressure systems are made up of large bodies of circulating air. In a high-pressure system, the high pressure is located at the center of the system, while the lower pressure is toward its outer reaches. High-pressure systems produce sunshine and clear weather. Low-pressure systems bring cloud cover and precipitation.

Some air masses stay the same for several days. Air pressure, temperature, and humidity remain steady within these air masses. A continental air mass is formed over a large stretch of land; a maritime air mass is formed over water. Cold temperatures produce polar air masses, and warm temperatures produce tropical air masses.

When air masses collide, they create weather fronts where major weather changes occur. There are four main types:

Cold front: When a colder air mass makes its way toward a warmer one, showers and thunderstorms result.

Warm front: When a warmer air mass moves toward a colder one, the result is extended periods of precipitation.

Stationary front: When a boundary formed between two air masses stalls, it causes light rain and cloudy skies.

Occluded front: When a faster-moving cold front meets a slower-moving warm front, some degree of precipitation will occur.

Some weather patterns result in severe weather, like thunderstorms, tornadoes, and hurricanes. Sometimes, weather can be so dangerous that it causes significant damage and even death.

Low-pressure systems form thunderstorms, which can develop quickly. Thunderstorms have three phases. The first is called the cumulus stage. During this period, the system's clouds develop, and updrafts (air currents that move skyward from the ground) occur. Once the cumulus clouds are formed, downdrafts (air currents that move from the direction of the sky down toward the ground) appear. This movement of air patterns results in thunderstorms, which usually weaken and dissipate within 30 minutes.

The updrafts and downdrafts in a thunderstorm create tiny ice crystals that are positively and negatively charged. When these particles interact, lightning is caused.

When thunderstorm updrafts begin rotating, tornadoes are likely to form. As the updrafts rotate, a spiral of swirling winds moves downward from the base of the thunderstorm, creating a funnel cloud. Once this cloud touches the ground, a tornado officially forms.

Hurricanes are perhaps the most destructive form of thunderstorms. A hurricane is about 150,000 times larger than a tornado. Hurricanes are similar to tornadoes in wind speed, but they form over the ocean, causing flooding and other severe destruction. Hurricanes gain power from warm water and will slowly lose momentum over land or colder water. Hurricanes are called typhoons in Asia. In Australia, they are called tropical cyclones.

IMPACT OF CLIMATE CHANGE

Climate change refers to the warming of Earth's atmosphere. It is also called global warming. Scientists believe that the actions of humans since the Industrial Revolution have caused global temperatures to increase by 1°C. While that doesn't seem like a lot, it actually has a major impact on people and animals.

The burning of fossil fuels is one of the major causes of climate change. When burned, these fuels release gases into the atmosphere, causing an invisible layer that traps the sun's heat on the planet's surface, slowly warming it. This is called the Greenhouse Effect.

Deforestation is another significant cause of climate change. One example of deforestation is the cutting down of the Amazon rainforest for wood, making palm oil, and clearing land for farming, roads, and oil mining.

The planet has gone through many different climate periods, including tropical climates and ice ages, which makes people wonder why climate change matters so much. If the temperature is increasing now, how is it different from the last time it increased? Greenhouse gases weren't involved the last time.

This time around, humans have been releasing these gases for more than a century, causing the temperatures to rise more rapidly. The result of climate change may include increased rainfall, rising sea levels, melting sea ice, and seasonal changes.

The effects on wildlife can already be seen with the major loss of Arctic Sea ice. Experts have found it is melting at about 4.7% per decade. Animals like the polar bear require the ice for several reasons, including resting after swimming for a long time. Additionally, apes in Indonesia are at risk because their rainforest habitats are continuously being cut down.

We've learned some important things in this chapter, including the effects of Earth's orbit and rotation. Now that we know how weather and climate change work, wrapping up our look at living things, let's move on to something related: the world of electricity and circuits.

CHAPTER FIVE:
ELECTRICITY AND CIRCUITS

Electricity is one of the most powerful forces on Earth. Depending on how it is used and controlled, it can cause extreme damage or power entire cities. Learning how it works is quite interesting and can help you know how to use it safely. Let's start by looking at the basics of electricity before defining and exploring what circuits are.

BASICS OF ELECTRICITY

To understand electricity, we need to look at the smaller side of things. We've already discovered what an atom is. These tiny little units have even smaller particles called protons and electrons. These tiny particles are always in a constant state of movement around one another. Protons always have positive charges, while electrons always have negative charges. Positive and negative charges are drawn to each other, while two positives or two negatives will drive one another away. These forces push and pull electrons from atom to atom, creating electricity.

Most objects, including people, have a neutral charge, which means there is a balance between the positive and negative charges. In other words, there is no pushing or pulling between the charges to generate electricity. Otherwise, everything would generate electricity all the time!

However, there are some cases in which an object can have a buildup of electrons. When two objects with this type of buildup come into contact, they can push and pull on each other as they are no longer neutral. When two objects have this push and pull due to extra electrons, it's called static electricity. When finally released, static electricity can cause some pretty wild effects, including simple sparks and entire lightning bolts.

One great example of static electricity is when you run a balloon through your hair. The friction creates extra electrons in your hair, which all try to push against each other. This creates the effect of your hair standing on end as each strand attempts to fly away from the rest.

An electric current contains moving electrons. Electric currents made by generators power everything in your home through wires. Wires connect to outlets so that when you plug in a device, the current runs from the wire through the outlet and into your device.

The Ancient Greeks completed the first studies on electric forces. Scientists later learned that electricity and magnetism are closely linked, developing ways to generate electricity with magnets.

CIRCUIT COMPONENTS AND PRINCIPLES

An electric circuit is a path for electricity to move along. It wasn't until the early 1800s that scientists learned how to channel a continuous flow of electricity through a circuit.

A circuit consists of a power source, plastic-coated metal wires, and the device that will use the electric current. All these parts must be connected to continue electricity to flow.

Most circuits also have switches. Flipping a switch on completes the circuit, allowing the electricity to flow through it to power the devices wired in. Flipping the switch in the other direction will break the circuit, ending the current flow.

There are two types of circuits: the series circuit, in which everything is set up in a loop with one piece right after the next.

The current flows from one part to the next in the loop. Additionally, for every device added, the current decreases in strength. If any single part of a series circuit burns out, the entire circuit will stop working.

A parallel circuit has multiple pathways, which means the electric current only partially flows through any given pathway at a time.

APPLICATIONS IN EVERYDAY LIFE

Electricity's primary household use is for heating and cooling purposes.

Of course, it's not just about your indoor temperature at home. Nearly everything you use has electricity at its heart, from your gaming devices to your computer to your lights.

In factories, all those big machines need a power source, and as you probably guessed, it's electricity. When the plants that manufacture various materials have a power outage, it can be a major problem for all the companies that depend on what they produce.

If you stop and look around you the next time you go out, you'll see electricity everywhere. The entire world runs on electricity from the streetlights to the movie theatre to the mall.

As always, learning about electricity can be quite shocking. Let's take our new knowledge of circuits and grow on that to learn about computers and technology in the next chapter.

CHAPTER SIX:
COMPUTERS AND TECHNOLOGY

Where would we be today without all the computers and technology we're used to turning to at a moment's notice? Homework would be a lot more difficult! We'd also be a bit more bored when we have free time. So, let's learn about what makes computers and technology great and the different parts that make them work.

BASICS OF COMPUTING

By now, you probably know what a computer is and have used one at least once, whether at home or school. But how does a computer work? At its most basic level, a computer processes, stores, and retrieves data. You've probably used one to play a game, do homework, or even take a test. They're also great for making videos and presentations.

When it comes to the critical parts of a computer, you need to know the difference between hardware and software. Hardware is any physical component of the computer, including the keyboard, mouse, and monitor. Software is like a specific set of directions that tells your computer how to do its job. Examples of software include video games, word processors, and web browsers.

There are many kinds of computers, including laptops and desktops. However, there are other types of computers, like ATMs and scientific calculators, to name two.

Desktop computers must be used in one location, preventing mobility. While a desktop isn't as convenient as a laptop or tablet, its hardware can be upgraded to accommodate your needs better than portable devices. Today, some TVs are even considered a type of computer. Smart TVs have apps allowing you to view online content, including your favorite streaming services. Other computers you may use include video game consoles and wearables like a smartwatch.

Personal computers have two operating systems: PC and Mac. The PC was first established by IBM in 1981. Today, most of these devices come with the Windows operating system. The Apple Corporation produces Macs. The first Macintosh computer debuted in 1984 and was the first model to have a graphic user interface. Macs use the Mac OS X operating system.

HARDWARE AND SOFTWARE COMPONENTS

Hardware makes up the computer and has a physical structure. Hardware can be broken down into two types: internal and external.

Internal hardware is everything inside your computer. The main piece is the motherboard. This printed circuit board is the central hub of the computer system. It holds the central processing unit (CPU) and other important pieces of the computer's internal hardware.

Your computer's CPU takes information and instructions from different programs to operate the computer and functions like the device's brain. The CPU's clock speed determines how well the computer performs and what level it works when processing data.

RAM is a temporary memory storage that lets programs access information immediately. This type of storage is wiped clean whenever you power down the computer. Other types of storage include hard disk drives, solid-state drives (SSDs), and optical drives. The hard drive can store permanent and temporary data in various formats. SSDs are not clear when the power is turned off, keeping all data permanently stored until you delete it. Optical drives are used to read discs.

Computers also require a heat sink, a device used to draw heat away from the most important components. Many parts of a computer will generate heat. When they become too hot, they can stop functioning. The heat sink will pull the heat off these parts, allowing them to operate efficiently. In most cases, the CPU puts out the most heat and will have a heat sink installed directly on top of it.

External hardware consists of the parts of the computer that allow you to input commands, give directions, and make the computer do what you need. A mouse and keyboard are the most commonly used external hardware. They can be wired or wireless, allowing you to interact with the computer directly. A microphone, camera, and speakers will enable you to use your computer for communication.

Software, on the other hand, is a term used to describe the programs, applications, and scripts that can be used to operate a computer. There are two main types: system and application software. The system software is designed specifically to operate the computer's hardware. Additionally, it creates a platform on which applications can run. Application software either performs a specific task or satisfies a need.

When computers were first created, software was preinstalled. In the 1980s, software was sold on external storage devices called floppy disks, which were large flexible disks. As technology advanced, floppy disks were replaced with CDs and DVDs. Today, most software is available for purchase and download online, eliminating the need for external storage devices.

The computer's operating system (OS) is the most common example of system software. This one piece of software manages all the other programs inside your computer, such as office suites, web browsers, and image modification programs.

While a computer can have many pieces of application software, none will work without an operating system. Web applications, however, just need the internet. If your device has a web browser with working internet, you can use these applications because their essential components are on the web server.

System software is always working in the background and is not something you will directly interact with. Instead, it ensures that your computer runs smoothly. As soon as you boot up your computer, system software begins to work and remains active until the device is powered down.

INTERNET AND NETWORKING

The Internet is a vast network that connects billions of computers globally. Initially developed in the 1900s, it was only meant for personal computers, limiting access to the home, office, school, or library. Since those days, it has changed a lot and is a lot quicker and easier to access.

No matter where you go today, you can check whatever you need on the internet using your smartphone, tablet, or TV. A long time ago, having access like this was only a dream. The start of the internet wasn't exactly what you'd call glamorous, but it paved the way for what we have today.

The first form of the internet, ARPANET, was created in the 1960s. In 1971, email was invented. Later in the 1970s, computers were ultimately connected by networks. Advances in technology were made to create routers, which were devices used to connect individual networks. With these advances, ARPANET would eventually become the internet.

The term hypertext was coined in the 1960s. It refers to the link between parts of a document or several documents. This invention became essential to creating the World Wide Web, which was established in the late '80s.

The World Wide Web is set up on individual pages and websites. To view these sites, you must use a web browser. Each website is created with a special language called hypertext markup language (HTML). Web browsers read and interpret the HTML code to allow you to view the website on your computer.

Whenever you use the internet, it's important to think about what you are making publicly available for the world to see. Anything you post or make accessible to others is called your digital footprint. To keep yourself safe, you need to closely monitor this information to prevent the wrong people from gaining access.

Many websites have chat boards where you can post messages or converse with other users. Many of these boards are visible to the general public. It's important to remember that not everyone is who they seem online. People can pretend to be someone they are not. Because of this, you should never agree to meet anyone when interacting with strangers in an online setting.

Any computer connected to a network must be protected from potential threats. Cybercrimes are criminal activities performed by individuals who use computers to do bad things, including phishing for information, hacking into other people's computers, or using malware.

Phishing typically uses an email created to look like a real email from someone you may know. A link in the email will then direct you to a website that asks for personally identifying information or financial information. Once this information is collected, cybercriminals can use it for all kinds of bad things, including stealing your identity.

Hacking is a serious crime that involves breaking through the security of someone else's computer system. By doing this, criminals can breach sensitive information, gain access to credit card numbers, personally identify information, and more. Some hackers have even gone so far as to try to hack the United States government's computer systems.

Malware can take over a computer, slowing its processes and damaging stored data. It can be sent to a computer via email or downloaded from an unsafe website.

You'll need to install anti-virus software and a firewall to ensure your computer stays safe while on the internet. Anti-virus software helps protect your computer from threats of various computer viruses as long as you regularly update it. A firewall filters all the data transmitted between the internet and your computer. It will block anything it finds to be unsafe.

While computers and technology are essential to our daily lives, using them correctly and safely is very important. Understanding how to stay safe while on the internet is one of the most important aspects of using a computer today. The same can be said for using smartphones and other mobile technology. In the next chapter, we'll explore these handy devices and learn how they can benefit us.

CHAPTER SEVEN: SMARTPHONES AND MOBILE TECHNOLOGY

Most people today have a smartphone or other mobile device that allows them to connect with the rest of the world, no matter where they are. Cell phones have come a long way from their initial clunky models. Additionally, they've gone from being able to make phone calls to essentially functioning as pocket-sized computers, allowing for browsing the internet, viewing social media, and playing games. Let's explore how these devices evolved into what we know and love today.

EVOLUTION OF MOBILE DEVICES

It might be hard to believe, but mobile phones weren't always as useful or easy to use as they are today. The very first mobile phone was clunky and weighed approximately 2.4 pounds. If you think your phone takes a long time to charge, consider this: This model would only work for 30 minutes of call time after being charged for 10 hours! The world's first mobile phone call was made in 1973 by Martin Cooper from Motorola, using this giant device. He called his competition Dr. Joel Engel, a Bell Labs engineer.

Around ten years after that first call, in 1983, the cell phone was made available for commercial purchase. Motorola released the DynaTac at a whopping $4,000 per phone. Unfortunately, this model was still heavy and clunky. This was a trait that all mobile phones would have until Motorola released new technology in 1989. The MicroTac introduced flip phone technology that was small enough to fit in a shirt pocket.

In the year 2000, Nokia became a huge cellular presence. This company's release of the Nokia 6000 series of cell phones marked the introduction of small models with durable, rectangular shapes that easily fit into pockets and the palm of one's hand. They were more affordable for the general public and allowed for internet browsing. Samsung also released important technology during this period. The Samsung SPH-I300 marked the dawn of touchscreen dialing.

T-Mobile released the Sidekick in 2002, providing a new way to craft messages that didn't involve T-9. This compact device had a full keyboard hidden behind the screen. When users pulled it out, they could use the phone like a mini-computer.

That same year, Sprint jumped on the bandwagon of advancing technology to release the Sanyo SCP-5300, a camera phone that sold for $400. When the camera phone was first released, it was in high demand. However, the focus stayed on advancing other aspects of the technology until much later.

In 2004, the RAZR was released. It had a sleek design and offered users a color screen. More than just a way to make a phone call, it became the ultimate fashion statement and was available in silver, black, blue, and pink.

Apple made major waves in the cell phone industry in 2007 with the first iPhone. At this point, phones were no longer just for communication—they became a way to perform essential daily tasks. The iPhone offered users touchscreen functionality, a virtual keyboard, and internet access through Safari. Despite the major advances in technology, the release of the BlackBerry greatly overshadowed the iPhone. Its instant messaging capability made it the most sought-after device of its time.

One year later, Apple launched its app store. At the start, it had 500 apps. In just the first week, over 10 million apps were downloaded by iPhone users. Android released its store a few months later with a mere 50 apps. Research In Motion soon followed with BlackBerry App World.

The iPhone 4 was released in 2010 and offered a battery that could keep up with the high demands of user activity. One year later, Apple advanced the technology further, releasing the iPhone 4S, which introduced Siri. Samsung also released newer technology during this period with the Galaxy Note. In 2015, Samsung pushed the limits again with the Edge series, whose screen wrapped around the phone's edges.

Since then, there has been a rapid release of models from various phone manufacturers, with Apple and Samsung leading the charge. Today, we're used to common features like biometric sign-ins and apps with facial recognition. Today, phones allow us to remotely control our smart home features, providing complete integration of all the technology we own. Advancements in artificial intelligence enable our phones to learn our behaviors and provide additional support, such as automating tasks, enhancing battery life, and enhancing security.

OPERATING SYSTEMS AND APPS

An operating system on a mobile device works a lot like that which runs a computer. You can do everything on your phone, from sending emails to searching the internet to using your favorite apps, just like on a full-size computer.

The three most commonly used operating systems for cell phones are Android, iOS, and Windows Mobile. Google is the mastermind behind Android, the world's most widely used mobile phone operating system. Apple created the iOS operating system for iPhones and iPads. The Microsoft Corporation launched Windows Mobile, allowing complete integration with the Windows computer operating system. It allows cell phone users to connect their devices to a monitor to enable use similar to that of a full desktop computer with a feature called Continuum.

Each of these operating systems offers users several benefits and advantages. While Android is considered to have the most flexibility, iOS is much more user-friendly. Windows Mobile has a smaller fan base but appeals to those who like features such as Continuum.

The earliest systems were very basic. They offered users limited functionality and did not compare to what we have available today. The late 2000s saw the launch of iOS and Android operating systems, marking a significant turning point in how mobile devices could be used. These operating systems offered an enhanced user experience with improved user interfaces, customization options, and advanced features. Every year since their initial release, these operating systems have improved in appearance and function. Today, they are significantly more powerful, packed with features, and a breeze for users to get a handle on.

A common feature among all mobile devices is apps. Snake was the first mobile app and was released in 1997. Third-generation (3G) mobile networks became available in 2000. These advanced networks made downloading larger apps a possibility. From there, smartphone manufacturers allowed third-party apps to be downloaded onto their phones, creating a brand-new industry. This enabled incredible changes in how users shop, travel, work, and play using mobile devices.

Mobile phones come with preinstalled apps that are generally required for the basic function of the phone, including text messaging, an internet browser, an email client, and more. Beyond that, users can download anything compatible they would like to use on their phone. Each manufacturer works with a specific app store, providing access to a world of options.

There are typically three types of apps: native, web-based, and hybrid. Native apps are customized to run off a specific operating system. This makes them more secure and faster than many alternatives. Additionally, they can interact with the mobile device's hardware.

Web-based apps rely on the device's browser to function. Because of this, they are generally slower and cannot be used when your phone is offline. However, they are compatible with any operating system.

Hybrid apps borrow characteristics from both native and web-based apps. They look and function a lot like native apps but lack their speed and power. They're also compatible with all operating systems.

In general, a mobile app will not have the same features and functionality as a full desktop version of the same app. This is due to its limited access to storage, processing power, and memory. Additionally, mobile apps are meant to be operated over mobile networks, which can be a challenge depending on your location and the dependability of your specific network. For instance, the network may not be as solid in rural settings as in a larger urban area.

IMPACT ON COMMUNICATION AND SOCIETY

Mobile devices have made communication much easier. Gone are the days when you had to be at home to receive a phone call or message from someone. Whether it was medical, job-related, or something equally important, you might have to sit at home all day waiting. The same was true for receiving emails.

Now, everything is in the palm of your hand. You can receive emails, phone calls, and text messages with a touch of your finger, and you can even sign important documents on your phone.

Improvements in technology have enhanced educational opportunities, too. A slew of mobile learning apps and educational content can be accessed through mobile devices. Additionally, these enhancements make mobile learning possible in areas where traditional schools may not be an option.

Nowadays, seeing a doctor through a mobile app is possible when you're too sick to make an in-person visit. In addition, technological advances have helped track global medical crises, such as the COVID-19 pandemic, alerting individuals to possible contact with infected individuals.

Each year, we see vast improvements in the world of mobile technology. It's anyone's guess where we'll be in a few years. In our next chapter, we will change things up a bit and switch to the science and technology behind flight and aerodynamics.

CHAPTER EIGHT:
FLIGHT AND AERODYNAMICS

Without flight and aerodynamics, travel options would be severely limited. Traveling by plane allows us to reach our destinations faster than other travel options. With all the improvements in flight technology, space exploration was inevitable. This final frontier offers an abundance of information, so let's look at how the fascinating world of flight works, both in the upper atmosphere and beyond.

PRINCIPLES OF FLIGHT

There's no doubt about it: Airplanes are huge. So, how do they manage to get into the air and stay up there? It all comes down to the basic principles of flight: lift, weight, drag, and thrust. They work together, creating a very delicate balance that determines where the aircraft will go. Lift and weight oppose one another; Drag and thrust do the same. However, it's a bit more complicated than that, but we will need to go into a bit of history to get to the heart of the matter.

Daniel Bernoulli was a renowned 18th-century physicist who studied fluid dynamics as well as fluids' movement and behavior. His most important contribution was a principle explaining the relationship between a fluid's velocity and pressure. This principle is very important to understanding how air moves around various objects, including the wings of an airplane.

As a plane moves through the sky, air flows over the wings and splits into two streams. The wings have two surfaces: one upper curved surface and one lower flat surface. One stream flows over the top and one under the bottom. Bernoulli's principle states that the air flowing over the top will increase velocity but decrease pressure. In turn, an area of higher pressure is created below the wing. The air pressure difference results in the force called *lift*, which allows for take-off and continued flight.

Before fully diving into lift, weight, drag, and thrust, we need to cover several important terms. The first is vectors. A *vector* is a value used to describe the location of something and provide the direction in which it is traveling, like a small arrow that indicates direction and distance. Pilots rely on vectors to ensure they fly the plane in the right direction. Vectors reveal where the plane is, where it's going, and how fast it's traveling. With this information, they can adjust their trajectory to ensure they safely arrive at the correct destination.

The other key term to know is resultant forces. A *resultant force* is the result of the fusion of two vectors. These forces matter because flights do not occur in a perfect space. There are many vectors at play during a flight that can affect how the plane moves. With both these terms in mind, it's time to look at the four forces that come together to create the principles of flight.

So, let's go back to lift. What is it exactly? It is a vector that moves perpendicular to the airflow around the plane. Additionally, its action occurs through the point where the total sum of pressure acts on the plane. The direct opposing force is weight, but it is influenced by air density, airspeed, wing size, and angle of attack. The lift vector's orientation will affect how the aircraft moves. For instance, if the plane were to turn upside down, the lift would move the plane downward instead of upward.

Weight is a vector that always points toward Earth's center and acts through gravity's center. It is affected by the total mass of the objects on the plane. Simply put, the more things a plane carries, the heavier it will be.

Like lift, drag works through that central point where the total sum of pressure is acting on the plane. However, it is also perpendicular to the lift vector's center. Its direction points toward the rear of the aircraft, and it is opposed by thrust. The amount of lift being produced, airspeed, air density, and the shape of the aircraft will all impact drag.

Thrust is a vector that always points forward in the engine's direction and acts through the center of thrust. It can be affected by altitude, engine RPM, air density, and airspeed.

For a plane to remain in steady flight, at a constant speed and altitude, the lift and weight vectors must be equal in magnitude. The thrust and drag vectors must also be perfectly aligned. To ascend, lift must exceed weight and thrust must exceed drag.

AIRCRAFT DESIGN AND TECHNOLOGIES

Aerospace engineering is a form of engineering that focuses on designing, creating, testing, and operating aircraft and spacecraft. The design process starts with a conceptual design phase. In this phase, designers use rough sketches to understand what will be needed for the aircraft's dimensions and configurations. This requires them to consider many factors, including wing location, the fuselage shape, and the engine size.

The next phase is the preliminary design phase. Engineers take the conceptual design and optimize it to fit all necessary parameters. They will use the designs to conduct specialized testing and complete required calculations. This phase is very important to the overall design and construction of the aircraft because engineers will look for any structural defects before the design moves to the third phase.

In the final stage, detail design, the physical aircraft is fabricated using the designs. This phase is used to create a fully functioning aircraft from the designs formed in the two previous phases. Flight simulations may be required to ensure the aircraft functions properly and is safe.

The first planes that were designed were nothing like what we know today. In fact, they were mere gliders—light crafts that soared great distances without needing an engine. Later, Orville and Wilbur Wright developed the first powered airplane that relied on propellers that used water-cooled engines to make them spin. Today, propellers are designed to provide a forward-direction lift. As they rotate, the air is deflected behind the propellers and then pushed forward on the blades, creating the thrust vector.

In 1937, the world of aviation surged forward with Frank Whittle's testing of the first jet engine. Unlike the common prop planes of the time, this model's engine sucked air through compressor blades that faced forward. The air then entered a combustion chamber, where it was combined with fuel and burned. The result was a superheated stream of gases being released from a tailpipe. This propelled the plane forward. In 1939, the world saw the first jet-propelled flight in Germany. Two years later, the British also developed their own jet engines.

Today, jet engines are typically reserved for the military. Regular commercial planes rely on a similar technology called turbofan engines. These also pull air through a forward-facing compressor but do not burn all the air in the chamber. Because of this, they produce fewer sound disturbances and are generally more efficient than regular jet engines.

The first airplanes ran on the same gas as cars. However, once the jet engine was developed, there was a need for improved fuel. While scientists and engineers first thought kerosene would be the ideal fuel option for planes, it had to be refined to prevent freezing or catching on fire.

Autopilot was developed to ensure that planes got to their destinations without crashing. The very first planes faced challenges of their own. Pilots were mostly tied up with ensuring they got off the ground, made their short flight, and landed successfully without crashing. As the technology keeping planes in the air improved, concerns were raised regarding the flight crew's ability to stay alert for long stretches of flying with the same scenery. While not every modern aircraft has an autopilot system, many do, ensuring the flight crew and passengers arrive at their destination safely.

Another important technology that is often taken for granted is air traffic control. These towers use surveillance radar to keep track of a plane's location and help guide it safely into the airport for a smooth landing. Additionally, most commercial planes carry a transponder programmed with key information, including the plane's identity, course, altitude, and speed. When the radar pings the plane, the transponder responds with this information.

SPACE EXPLORATION

When you think of space exploration, it's only natural to think of the moon landing with astronauts in big, puffy space suits. However, in today's world, spacecraft can also be unattended, with robotic creations gathering data to send back to scientists and researchers on Earth. Spacecraft is a general term that refers to many things, including satellites, space stations, and probes.

A space probe is an unmanned craft with just enough velocity to exit Earth's gravitational pull to orbit the planet. Alternatively, a deep-space probe is sent well beyond our Earth-moon system. When this type of probe is sent to explore another planet, such as Mars, it's also referred to as a planetary probe. A space station will be launched if there is a need for an extended stay in space. It is designed to support human life for a longer period.

When it's time for a spacecraft to launch into space, it must combat the forces of Earth's gravitational pull. A spacecraft requires a launch vehicle equipped with a rocket to enter Earth's orbit. As the rocket drives the spacecraft further away from the planet's surface, gravity has less and less of an effect. An interesting fact is that if a spacecraft is launched completely perpendicular to the Earth's surface, it will not break free from the gravitational pull and instead fall back to the ground. At a key moment, its velocity vector must be turned parallel to the planet's surface.

It takes a lot of force to break free from the gravitational hold of the planet. To achieve this, scientists and engineers developed a process called staging. This requires two or more rocket systems to be used when launching a spacecraft. They are mounted in a linear sequence and ignited from the rearmost position first.

Spacecraft have four general flight trajectories. The first of these is a sounding rocket. This trajectory allows for data collection at 28-100 miles (45-160 kilometers). The process uses single-stage or multi-stage vehicles launched almost completely vertically. Once each rocket stage burns all its fuel, the payload section will continue its upward movement until it loses all momentum due to gravity and begins its descent. In general, the payload will have an attached parachute that allows for its collection and reuse.

Earth orbit is the next trajectory. This typically requires that the spacecraft be launched vertically before its trajectory is tilted to be parallel to the surface of the planet. This tilt must occur when the craft reaches orbital velocity, which is the speed that allows the spacecraft to finally break free from Earth's pull. At this time, all rockets shut down. When the spacecraft reaches an altitude of 125 miles (200 kilometers), it requires a speed of 18,000 miles (29,000 kilometers) per hour to orbit Earth.

The Earth's escape trajectory allows for objects to fully break free from gravity. If you've ever seen videos of the moon landing, this is a perfect example of an Earth escape. In this situation, special calculations were made to shoot the shuttle past the moon, loop it back around the far side, and slow it down to fall into the moon's gravitational pull. Similar practices have been put into place to make unmanned craft landings on other planets.

Planetary trajectory involves sending a spacecraft to another planet and having it orbit the planet. To do this, calculations and research must be completed to identify how the spacecraft can be slowed correctly to be captured by the planet's gravitational pull. Initially, the spacecraft will use its onboard propulsion system to fire it into a wild elliptical-shaped orbit around the target planet. As the spacecraft makes several orbits, the drag created by gravity will transform the orbit into a circular shape, allowing for the mission to be completed.

Navigating in space can be a bit complicated. After all, no one is actually on those long-distance missions. Traveling from Earth to any point in space isn't as simple as moving in a straight line. Many forces in space can affect how the spacecraft moves. So, scientists and engineers developed a navigational system based on inertial guidance, which is a system that continuously monitors acceleration, position, and velocity.

Because inertial guidance systems are imperfect, they can experience small errors. The problem is that these errors will build up over time, eventually guiding the spacecraft off course. Because of this, many spacecraft sent on planetary missions are also equipped with a star tracker. This special device contains a telescope programmed to maintain coverage on three specific stars, allowing the tracker to always know where the spacecraft is. Some are even equipped with the technology to allow human flight controllers to manually adjust the trajectory to keep the spacecraft on course.

Flight and aerodynamics have certainly changed a lot of things for the entire world. Without them, we'd still be limited in travel and information on what lies beyond the horizon. In our next chapter, we'll learn how architecture and engineering work.

CHAPTER NINE:
ARCHITECTURE AND ENGINEERING

Architecture and engineering are closely related fields used in combination for designing, developing, and constructing buildings, infrastructure, and machines. Architecture focuses on creating beautiful exteriors, while engineering strives to design safe, secure structures. The combination ensures that the resulting designs are attractive and long-lasting. Here's a look at how these two fields work together.

STRUCTURAL DESIGN AND MATERIALS

Civil engineering is the specific branch of engineering that deals with the creation of strong, stable, and usable structures. Structural design is a subcategory of this branch. When the goal is to plan a visually appealing project, a structural engineer will partner with an architect. All the most famous buildings you've heard of around the world have a special structural design that keeps them from collapsing and is well hidden behind their beautiful exteriors.

During the structure's design process, these engineers use structural analysis and other important calculations to ensure they are developing a building that will be structurally dependable before the construction site is ever prepared. You can almost think of it as the structural engineer transforming the architect's ideas into something real instead of just drawings on paper.

There are two main types of structural design: rigid frame and concrete shell. A rigid frame design applies to a building constructed from a framework with welded joints. The columns and beams in this design can withstand a certain amount of movement and bending. A concrete shell lacks those internal beams and columns; It is typically in the shape of an oval.

When designing a building, several important forces and loads must be considered. The first is *shear*, the stress placed on the building as the structure moves in different directions. Next is *tensile*, the force on any part of the structure that can cause elongation or breaking. Third, *compressive* refers to the downward force on the building. This includes its own weight combined with the weight of everything in it.

In certain locations, structural engineers will specialize in structures that are resistant to certain conditions. Some areas of the world are particularly at risk for certain environmental hazards, such as high winds or earthquakes. Engineers can create structures that resist the forces created by these hazards.

The engineer must focus on several important requirements when a structure is in the design process. These include safety, strength, serviceability, aesthetics, and economy. The stability factor ensures the structure will remain standing without overturning, sliding, or excessively moving. Strength keeps the building from collapsing due to its own weight. For a structure to be serviceable, it must offer good performance when carrying a load. In other words, it should be able to handle things like vibrations that occur within acceptable limits, like nothing happened. Aesthetics are an optional feature, depending on the project, as not every structure requires a beautiful appearance. Safety, strength, and serviceability should be achievable within the budget, delivering the economic piece of the puzzle.

During design, structural engineers determine three important loads that will affect the structure once it is constructed. The first is called *live loads*. These loads include occupants and their belongings in buildings or cars on bridges. *Dead loads* are just the loads caused by the physical structure. *Environmental loads* are those caused by different environmental conditions, such as snow, earthquakes, and hurricanes. These loads will be different in every location.

There are five materials that are most commonly used in construction. Concrete is known as a composite material, which means it's made of two or more parts. The first part is a fine aggregate material. The second part is a binding material, which is often cement and water. Once mixed and poured, concrete must cure for seven days. After that, it takes another 28 days for it to reach its maximum strength. When used in construction, reinforcing concrete with steel is a common practice. Because it is so easy to use, concrete is applied to many different projects, including bridges, commercial buildings, residential buildings, foundations, and sewers.

The explosion of skyscraper construction was mostly due to the identification of steel as a reliable reinforcement material. It has impressive strength and excellent functionality. It's a popular material because it's lightweight and easy to work with. In addition to this, it's cheaper to ship than a lot of other materials, making it more affordable to use. Plus, steel won't bend until a massive amount of force is applied to it. Even after being bent, it will still retain its structural properties. It is because of these properties that steel is used to create the structural frameworks of the tallest buildings.

Wood is one of the oldest construction materials. It's a renewable resource, can be easily molded into different shapes, is durable, and doesn't cost a lot. Wood also pairs well with other materials like steel and marble, allowing for beautiful, elaborate constructions. It is often used in the entire construction of a building, from the floor to the roof, and provides thermal and acoustic insulation.

Stone as a building material dates back to ancient times and is what most of the world's ancient buildings were constructed from. Today, it's commonly used to build walls and flooring. Its texture, ranging from smooth to rough, allows it to be used for many different functions. The major downside to stone is its weight. Because it is so heavy, it's challenging to move, especially over long distances. It is also a poor insulator for colder climates.

The masonry building process uses various types of bricks to construct buildings. Bricks can be made from many different materials such as concrete that has been reinforced by steel. One reason masonry is so popular as a building material is that it is fire-resistant. It is also strong enough to be used in load-bearing walls, including in multi-story buildings.

URBAN PLANNING AND SUSTAINABLE ARCHITECTURE

Urban planning is the division of the government that is responsible for the development of cities and towns. For years, urban planners were relied upon to determine how these locations would grow due to increasing populations. More recently, the focus has shifted to determining what to do with the vacant space left as more people move to rural settings.

In the late 19th century, most cities were dirty and overcrowded, leading to Illnesses like typhoid, influenza, cholera, and yellow fever. At this time, urban or city planners were called upon to solve the problem of widespread illness. Their solution was to move the residents farther from industrial areas. This brought about the creation of the laws known as zoning ordinances. These laws keep business districts and residential districts separate.

The major flaw in this plan was the sudden increase in reliance on cars for transportation. This caused a rise in air pollution and made walking to complete errands quite a challenge. In addition to these problems, city planning has been linked to a decrease in the overall health and wellness of the general population due to decreased physical activity and heavier reliance on driving to get where you need to go.

Around the world, many cities are making moves to create bike-friendly cities. Copenhagen, Munich, and Vienna are just a few that have closed down entire streets to automobile traffic. Other cities, like London, require drivers to pay a toll to enter the city. In Chicago, special bike lanes have been created to protect cyclists from cars driving past them.

Other cities have embraced the concept of mixed-use communities. Instead of strict zoning, these communities allow for housing, shops, and public transportation all in one area, minimizing the need for driving.

As cities become less populated, city planners are considering ways to incorporate community gardens. Urban gardening has become a popular concept in recent years as more people want to buy their produce from local sources. These spaces also allow community members to gain a sense of ownership in their neighborhoods. Working to maintain these spaces brings people together.

Along with urban planning, there is a strong move toward making communities more sustainable through architecture. Sustainable architecture refers to buildings specifically designed and constructed to limit how much of an impact we have on our environment. Buildings constructed this way use less energy and water over time and are made from fewer toxic materials than alternative options.

Sustainable architecture offers many benefits, including reducing harmful greenhouse gas emissions and conserving valuable natural resources. These buildings are often eco-friendly and equipped with solar power to provide clean, renewable energy. Some of them rely on natural heating, cooling, and ventilation systems. Most use rainwater harvesting techniques to limit water usage. Greywater is the used water that comes from your washing machine, kitchen sink, and shower. Methods are set in place to re-use this water for things like cleaning. The overall goal of sustainable architecture is to create a structure that produces at least the same amount of energy as it uses daily.

These buildings also feature renewable materials like bamboo, soy, cork, and hemp. In addition, they use eco-friendly insulating materials. Interestingly, sustainable architecture has alternative materials to replace concrete and plastic. Hempcrete is made of lime, hemp, and water and can take the place of concrete in buildings. Algae-based bioplastics that can easily take the place of mass-produced conventional options.

INNOVATIONS IN CONSTRUCTION

Around 100 years ago, construction was significantly different. Homes were typically small, lacked reinforcements, and had above-ground foundations. Building materials were as varied as the styles of homes. After World War II, more affordable materials became a priority. Homes were more frequently constructed with cheaper materials that were also more efficient.

Predesigned or "prefab" homes became a common option because of their efficiency and affordability. Construction teams did not have to complete elaborate builds, allowing them to repeat straightforward steps and build homes rapidly. Prefab homes are still used today, and there are various styles, from basic to luxury.

Another innovation that sped up the construction process was the introduction of framing packages. Instead of constructing everything on-site, builders could order kits with specific components of the building's structure pre-cut, labeled, and ready to be assembled. Instead of cutting each piece individually, the crew can unload the materials from the delivery truck and immediately begin piecing them together, saving hours of construction time.

As computer technology has advanced, the construction industry has jumped on board. Access to digital designs allows a designer or architect's thoughts and ideas to be shared before and during construction projects. This allows for greater customer collaboration and eliminates the waiting period for permits and documents.

In the past, working without personal protective gear on a construction site was considered a symbol of strength and fearlessness. As improvements were made across the board, safety became a significant concern. Rules and regulations were established, and essential gear was developed to ensure all construction workers had access to safety equipment.

The world of architecture and engineering is ever-changing, and there's no telling where we'll be in a few more decades. Now that we've explored this interesting field, let's move on to recycling and sustainability.

CHAPTER TEN:
RECYCLING AND SUSTAINABILITY

As the world has advanced in technology, waste management practices have become an important focus. Unfortunately, over the centuries, humankind has produced a lot of waste, which has filled landfills and polluted natural resources. Because of this, increased efforts have been placed on recycling and sustainable practices.

WASTE MANAGEMENT AND RECYCLING PROCESSES

Without waste management, we would have nowhere for our trash to go. The process involves the collection by waste management personnel, transport to waste management facilities, treatment based on the type of waste, and final disposal. Waste can be liquid, gas, or solid; each form requires different handling and management procedures.

Waste can directly impact human health, especially when it's hazardous. Biomedical waste is produced in healthcare facilities and can result from other situations. Exposure to this type of waste can spread diseases. Radioactive waste can destroy entire towns when not managed correctly. Because of the risks, all waste must be properly managed. This ensures it will not enter the groundwater or contaminate food and water supplies.

Waste management focuses on protecting human health and the environment from the dangerous effects different types of waste can have. However, waste management practices differ around the world. Effectively managing waste is essential to the healthy development of cities. Unfortunately, it is an expensive process to complete correctly. Because of this, developing countries often struggle to manage their waste efficiently.

Two common waste disposal methods are placing the waste in landfills or incinerating it. Once a landfill has been filled, the area over it may be repurposed to include housing. Incineration is a controversial method of disposal. While it effectively manages solid, nonhazardous waste, it can also be used to eliminate biomedical waste. However, it has the potential to produce a lot of emissions that can damage human health and the environment.

Recycling is a waste management process that takes certain waste products and reuses them. These products can include plastic bottles, paper, and plastic bags. This benefits the environment because plastic is not biodegradable and does not break down over time. Instead, it remains solid waste. When these items are recycled, they are broken down in a recycling center and repurposed into other products. This prevents them from being sent to landfills or becoming litter.

Many materials are eligible for recycling. However, the exact items that recycling facilities will accept depend on the country and city where you live. Some also offer money in exchange for recycling efforts. Different facilities will have different capabilities when it comes to what they can recycle.

ENVIRONMENTAL IMPACT OF CONSUMER CHOICES

What you buy and how you use it are part of the choices you make as a consumer. These choices can have a powerful impact on the environment. When you consume or use goods, it doesn't always have bad effects. It's when you overconsume that your impact on the environment becomes negative. The more products you consume, the more resources are used, and the more emissions produced.

As you make choices as a consumer, focus on sustainability. You and your family can have a major impact on the environment by making a few important decisions. First, when you want to buy something, consider whether you need it. Determine what it's made of and what long-term effects it will have if you discard it. Remember, plastic will never break down on its own and can harm the environment.

Second, consider how and where the product is made. Certain manufacturing processes produce a lot of pollution. By purchasing that product, you are enabling this pollution to continue. In addition, if the product is made in another country, it must travel a lot to get to the store where you'll buy it. Long-distance shipments produce excessive emissions that harm the environment.

Finally, you should consider what it costs to make the product. For instance, evaluate how many resources and energy is consumed during production. You should also consider what types of waste are produced due to its manufacture.

With a greater focus on sustainability when making purchases, consumers can have a significant positive impact on the environment.

SUSTAINABLE PRACTICES

You can practice sustainability right from home by not purchasing disposable items. Typically, these end up in landfills after you throw them out. If they're recyclable, they consume a lot of resources and energy to break them down and repurpose them.

Here's an interesting fact: Food waste doesn't break down like you'd expect it to in a landfill. Instead of the typical decomposition that occurs when the food is exposed to oxygen, it must break down anaerobically. Because of this, something as simple as a head of lettuce can take over two decades to break down! Even worse is that it will produce methane gas, which is more damaging than carbon dioxide. Because of this, it's important to reduce food waste as much as possible.

A good majority of the plastic waste in the world comes from packaging. An estimated 40% of all plastic produced is used to package products we purchase. By buying items with less packaging, you can make a strong impact on the environment by decreasing the amount of waste you produce.

Recycling is very important. By looking into the proper procedures and teaching your family and friends, you can help prevent excessive waste from reaching landfills. Something important to remember is that if an item is not recyclable and you place it in a recycling bin, you may have just contaminated the entire bin. This results in all the materials being sent to a landfill because they can no longer be repurposed.

Effective waste management and recycling are essential to preserving our natural world. By practicing sustainability and making good consumer choices, you can help support the environment. In the next chapter, we'll explore the world of transportation systems.

CHAPTER ELEVEN:
TRANSPORTATION SYSTEMS

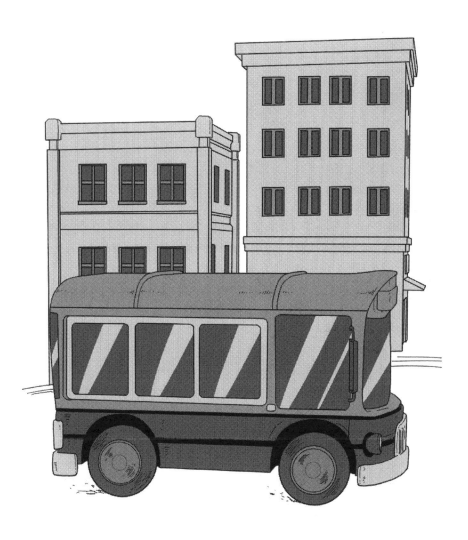

Transportation is essential, as it allows us to get from point A to point B much more easily and quickly than walking. Whether you ride in a car, take the train, or fly in an airplane, today's technology is quite impressive. Since the initial introduction of these transportation methods, great strides have been made to improve them, making them safer and more efficient for everyone.

AUTOMOTIVE TECHNOLOGIES

The automobile made its grand entrance on the scene in France in 1769. Germany introduced the automobile in the late 1800s. However, it was the Americans who took over the industry during the 20th century. The Mercedes was the first modern motorcar to have all the essentials, developed in 1901. It had a 35-horsepower engine and could travel at a speed of 53 miles per hour. Despite having the most integrated factory in Europe, the manufacturer, Daimler Motoren Gesellschaft, could only produce less than 1,000 of these cars yearly with its 1,700 employees.

In stark contrast to the superior European design of motorcars, the 1901–1906 Oldsmobile was a three-horsepower motorized buggy. However, it was much more affordable at $650, making it accessible to middle-class Americans. Additionally, the factory output was significantly greater at 5,508 units in 1904. The first decade of the 20th century was focused on delivering the quality of the Mercedes at the price of the Oldsmobile.

The year 1908 was big for the American automotive industry. It marked the introduction of Ford's Model T and the establishment of General Motors. Ford was the leader in pairing affordable pricing with modern design. After 1906, Ford made advancements in its factory to meet the daily demands of 100 car deliveries. Henry

Ford established mass production techniques used at his new factory that opened in 1910 in Highland Park, Michigan. Then, in 1913–1914, he introduced the moving assembly line. Naturally, Ford's advanced industry techniques quickly caught on and spread throughout the United States, with American car manufacturers rapidly jumping aboard.

Major advancements were made by the 1920s with the introduction of hydraulic brakes, the self-starter, and the synchromesh transmission. Further innovations came in the 1930s with the advent of the automatic transmission and drop-frame construction. During the Great Depression, automotive sales and advancements fell off. They picked back up during World War II with the production of military vehicles and critical military items. However, it wasn't until after the war that the demand for civilian automobiles returned.

Post-war production in the United States severely lacked quality. In the mid-1960s, American automotive production was so poor that cars featured an average of 24 defects each. The worst part about it was that many were safety related. In 1966, federal stipulations were established regarding automotive safety requirements. Additionally, regulations were passed in 1965 and 1970 regulating harmful emissions.

Around that time, German and Japanese manufacturers gained a significant foothold in the American automotive industry, delivering top-quality, fuel-efficient cars. Because of their influence, American automakers had to step up their game and introduce smaller cars that could compete with similar features.

Since then, incredible features have been developed, including power windows and steering. In addition, today's vehicles are equipped with safety features, including airbags, backup camera assist, and blind spot indicators. Research and development are focused on what improvements can be made to increase driver safety and comfort, including autonomous driving abilities. With all the advancements, there's no telling where the automotive industry will head next.

RAIL AND MASS TRANSIT

Trains are composed of several important pieces. These include the locomotives that pull them, the cars that carry people and freight, the switches and signals that direct traffic, and the tracks the train moves on. So, how do all these parts work together to make trains safe and efficient?

In most cases, the locomotive takes the frontmost position of the train. Behind it, the passenger train cars are linked in a row. As the locomotive moves forward, it pulls the cars behind it along the track, designed to steer where the train goes. It's important to remember that more than one train can travel on a track simultaneously. When this happens, the railroad uses switches and signals to keep everyone safe from accidents.

The locomotive has a very important job. It takes the fuel the engineer provides and transforms it into kinetic energy, or the energy of motion. The fuel can be several different things, including diesel fuel, wood, or coal. The original locomotives relied on steam as their fuel source but were eventually replaced with those that moved more efficiently with other types of fuel. Today, modern trains rely on electrical power. The tracks have a third rail supplying the electricity for these models. These trains are commonly found in subway systems.

The engineer uses three important parts when operating the train: the reversing gear, the throttle, and the brake. The reversing gear allows the train to travel in reverse while the throttle manages the speed. As you might expect, the brake slows and stops the train's movement. No matter what engine is used, the system's brakes include air and hand brakes.

Mass transit involves moving large groups of people from one point to another. This is often completed using trains or buses. In large metropolitan areas, subway systems often run the trains underground, saving space and making travel more efficient. Because so many people travel together, the costs of transportation are reduced.

These transportation options generally run on a set timetable and make designated stops along the route. Travelers can easily plan their trips based on where the transit will stop, saving money on driving and limiting their environmental impact.

MARITIME AND AIR TRANSPORTATION

Maritime transportation refers to travel by sea. It can be the movement of people or cargo, depending on the type of ship. With the advancement of air transportation, traveling by water for passengers is generally reserved for short distances or luxury cruises. Water transport is much more affordable, but the downside is how long it takes for ships to travel from one country to the next.

Depending on the type of ship, different types of loads can be carried. Some hold large containers, while others hold bulk, nonperishable foods. Generally, any foods that will spoil during the lengthy trips will not be shipped via boat. The average port-to-port time from a European country to the United States is 10–12 days.

While sea travel was once solely powered by the wind, today, it can harm the environment. Ships produce greenhouse gas emissions and have the potential to cause oil and fuel leaks in the waters they travel through. While technological advancements have improved the shipping process's overall efficiency, they have resulted in potentially dangerous environmental problems.

Not so long ago, the world depended on shipping to transport goods and mail worldwide. It was also the only way for people to cross the oceans. When air transportation became available and more widespread, it quickly became the preferred method of transport.

Weeklong trips were dramatically reduced, allowing perishable items to be safely transported. Important news could be sent via the mail to receive a fast response. Traveling also became significantly more convenient. Despite the convenience, not all goods can be shipped by air. Due to their explosive nature, some hazardous materials must always be shipped by ground or boat transport.

Like maritime transport, air transport is also a significant contributor to climate change. Planes produce greenhouse gas emissions and burn non-renewable fossil fuels.

With so many ways to travel, it makes getting around a breeze. Now that you know the ins and outs of these transportation systems, let's look at how communication networks function.

CHAPTER TWELVE: COMMUNICATION NETWORKS

Communication networks are the key to keeping society connected. They come in different forms, from the internet to wireless technologies. These networks are essential for work to be completed efficiently, as they allow for file sharing across great distances in mere seconds. Not only that, but you can easily communicate with anyone anywhere instead of waiting months for a response like our ancestors had to. So, let's look at how the different types of communication networks function.

INTERNET INFRASTRUCTURE

To fully understand the internet and how it works, you must first know what a network is. In simple terms, it's a bunch of connected computers that can send data between them. The Internet consists of many interconnected networks. Computers can communicate with other computers in their own network or with those in another network because of the capabilities of the Internet. These connections are made possible through radio waves, wires, and cables. As data is transmitted, it is transformed into electrical pulses called bits. Bits are transmitted from one computer to the next at the speed of light, making communication nearly instantaneous.

It's important to note that the internet doesn't have a central control point. Instead, it functions based on the concept of a distributed networking system, which means it does not depend on a single device to operate. Any machine capable of sending and receiving data according to the network specifications can be part of the internet. Because of this setup, individual machines can be connected and disconnected from the internet without affecting how they function.

The internet's function comes down to two primary concepts: packets and protocols. Packets are small pieces of larger messages, and they contain data. In addition to this data, they also contain valuable information about that data. The information about the packet is placed at its front. This allows the receiving machine to know what to do with it. As data is sent over the internet, smaller packets are formed and broken down into bits. The packets are transmitted to the correct location, where the receiving machine reassembles them into the complete message to use the data correctly.

A protocol is like a standard operating procedure. Not all computers communicate the same way. For instance, Macs and Windows PCs have different operating systems, which can make it challenging for them to communicate. Protocols offer standardized ways of interpreting data so that these different systems can easily transmit information to one another. There are various types of protocols to handle different tasks. Some ensure packets arrive in order, while others allow packets to travel from network to network.

Some physical devices are also required to make the internet work. Routers are responsible for sending the packets from network to network. They ensure the packets travel in the right direction to the correct places. Switches are used to connect different devices that are all on the same network. They forward packets to the correct devices within the network.

SATELLITE COMMUNICATION

A satellite is an object located in a planet's orbit. It can naturally occur, such as on a moon or other planet. Alternatively, it can be an artificially created satellite launched into the planet's orbit for technological or scientific purposes. In the case of communication, many artificial satellites are launched into Earth's orbit.

These devices make the transmission and relay of information possible on a global scale. You might be surprised to hear that you use some kind of satellite communication every day. Whether you watch television, use high-speed Wi-Fi, or ride in the car while your parents use their GPS, you're using a form of this communication.

The process of satellite communication involves three parts: uplink, transponder, and downlink. To send a message, the source, such as a television broadcasting network, will send an uplink to a specific satellite. This is also called transmitting a signal. In the transponder stage, the satellite receives the signal, boosts its signal strength, changes its frequency, and relays it to the correct station on Earth. The downlink is the final step in which transmitters send those signals to Earth.

It's also possible to have two-way satellite communication. In this setup, two stations on Earth transmit and receive messages via the same satellite; they will each have an uplink and a downlink.

Satellite access stations are required on the ground to complete the message network. These stations send and receive messages on Earth and can be flat panels or dishes. All information is processed at these stations before being sent to its final location.

There are four types of satellites. They include highly elliptical orbit (HEO), medium Earth orbit (MEO), low Earth orbit (LEO), and geostationary Earth orbit (GEO). An HEO satellite will vary in its elevation above the Earth's surface, depending on where it's at in its orbit. Two HEO satellites must be in orbit together to ensure all connectivity is seamless.

MEO satellites are frequently used to power GPS systems and offer an alternative internet option for remote areas where installing other options is impossible. LEO satellites are small compared to the others and require many units to be in orbit to be effective globally. They're used for 5G networking, emergency response, maritime communications, tourism, and government networks. GEO satellites move so slowly that they look like they're not moving. They require three satellites in orbit to provide global coverage and are used in disaster response, inflight Wi-Fi, and uncrewed aerial vehicles.

WIRELESS TECHNOLOGIES

Wireless technology allows the transmission of signals or messages from one location to another without needing wiring or optic fibers. "Wireless" is often used to refer to communication that can be completed without these wires.

When data is transmitted wirelessly, it is sent from one location to another through electromagnetic waves. To keep things simple, these waves are called signals. The signal's source is called the transmitter. An oscillator will generate the signal as a periodic wave at this transmitter. This signal travels through the transmitter's wires and up through its antenna. The antenna is also an electrical conductor, so the signal will continue toward its tip. From there, the antenna converts the electric current into an electromagnetic wave.

In most cases, the signal doesn't travel in a straight line to its destination. Instead, the antenna will transmit it in several directions. The resulting waves can bounce off different surfaces, like buildings, or scatter when they hit small objects, like a toy.

Eventually, the waves reach the receiver, which will receive them all as one unified signal.

Today, we rely on a lot of different wireless technologies. Our cell phones are likely at the top of the list. Think about your games and computer. Do you use wireless controllers, keyboards, or a mouse? They all work with the same principles. Most of us also use wireless connectivity for our internet connections, as computers have been upgraded to connect to the network without a physical cable.

With this look at the different types of communication, you have a whole new understanding of how you can interact with the rest of the world. In the next chapter, we'll change gears by learning about cooking and food processes.

CHAPTER THIRTEEN:
COOKING AND FOOD
PROCESSES

Whether you've helped cook dinner or simply watched your parents do it, you know there's much more to it than just throwing some stuff in a pot. There's science behind making a meal. You can think of it like artistry that involves chemistry and nutrition. Let's learn how the process works so you can help in the kitchen next time!

CULINARY CHEMISTRY

Cooking is a truly transformative process. You start with a batch of ingredients and end with something good to eat. Cooking involves chemical reactions that change the food from one state to another. This can happen through emulsification or manipulation. Emulsification mixes two liquids that normally would not combine due to their chemistries. Manipulation can include changing the temperature, surface area, or concentration of ingredients.

Freezing can be used as a preservation technique or as part of the food preparation process. However, freezing can change the quality of the food, as it causes the formation of ice crystals. While freezing one time will likely have little effect on the food, repeated thawing and freezing will typically affect the texture and flavor of food.

Heating is another transformation process. Heating food makes it more palatable and safer to eat in the case of meat. Additionally, when you apply heat to food, it generally brings out the flavor. Cooking destroys harmful bacteria that may sicken people. Once a food is cooked, it must stay hot to prevent those same bacteria from returning.

Heat travels in different ways. When cooking, we typically use conduction, convection, and radiation. *Conduction* is the transfer of heat from a solid object to another object in direct contact with it. Consider making a pot of macaroni and cheese. First, you must boil the water. To do this, you place the water in a pot, which is in direct contact with the burner on the stove. The pot heats from contact with the burner and then conducts heat into the water until it boils. The same thing happens when cooking meat. The outside of the meat cooks first and conducts heat toward the center.

FOOD PRESERVATION AND PROCESSING

Inside all living plants and animals are tiny organisms called microorganisms. As long as the living thing is healthy and alive, these microorganisms stay at a healthy level. Once a plant or animal dies, certain microorganisms rapidly increase in number, including yeast, bacteria, and mold. This increase can cause food to spoil. As the food spoils, it loses nutrients, changes texture, develops an altered flavor, and emits an unpleasant odor. If you eat spoiled food, you can get sick.

Food preservation and processing methods date back to ancient times; for example, in cold climates, people would freeze food in the snow. In warm climates, sun exposure was used to dry foods.

Drying is the process of extracting the moisture from food. This is highly effective because microorganisms require this moisture for survival. Once you remove moisture, food takes longer to spoil. Since the ancient practice of sun drying, technology has advanced to allow for different types of drying. Today, machines are used to dry fruits and vegetables, especially in factories. Meats are often smoked dry, which can take several days.

Another commonly used food preservation technique is fermentation. It's a required process to manufacture cheese, beer, wine, bread, and more. It works by stopping the growth of those harmful organisms that cause food to spoil and allowing other microorganisms to grow more easily. These harmless microorganisms produce enzymes that break the food down into chemicals. Once this process is complete, the food will not spoil as easily.

Refrigerating and freezing are two common types of food preservation. Chilling or freezing food greatly slows the production of microorganisms that cause spoiling. Before modern-day refrigeration was developed, people used icehouses and iceboxes. These insulated structures contained ice and were used to keep food cold as long as possible. Mechanical refrigeration was developed in the 1800s, enabling the transportation of food without spoiling.

Canning uses heat to preserve food. The high temperatures kill the microorganisms, helping prevent spoiling. Once the food is heated, it's placed into vacuum-sealed canning jars. Canning was largely developed in the 1800s and was adopted by Louis Pasteur, who identified the process of treating food with heat to reduce the presence of microorganisms. This is known as pasteurization.

When you purchase food at the store, whether in cans or refrigerated, chemicals are typically added to it to prolong the freshness of the food. These preservatives include honey, sugar, vinegar, and ascorbic acid.

NUTRITIONAL SCIENCE

Food and nutrition are essential for your healthy growth and development. Since the 19th century, the primary focus on human nutrition has been macronutrients, which include fats, proteins, and carbohydrates. It wasn't until 1926 that the first vitamin was identified and isolated. This vitamin was thiamine, a B vitamin. In 1932, vitamin C was identified and isolated. At this same time, it was initially documented that vitamin C is medically beneficial in combatting scurvy. With that in mind, nutritional science examines how the food we eat affects our overall well-being.

With the discovery of those first vitamins came the trend of producing synthetic vitamins. These manufactured nutrients were then used to help individuals battle nutrient deficiencies. This is a primary focus of nutritional science today because of how important vitamins are to our health.

Since the 1990s, nutritional science has focused on battling the challenges of poor diet. Researchers have emphasized ways to help people manage their weight and improve their nutritional education to live longer, more fulfilling lives.

When it comes to food, it's important to use proper handling techniques to prevent getting sick. In addition, eating the right combination of nutrients is essential to getting the most from your food. With this basic understanding of cooking and food preservation, you now have the knowledge needed to embrace a safer, healthier lifestyle. In the next chapter, we'll focus on sound and acoustics.

CHAPTER FOURTEEN:
SOUND AND ACOUSTICS

At its most basic level, sound is anything that can be perceived by the sense of hearing. Ultimately, a vibration travels through a solid, liquid, or gas as an acoustic wave. Understanding how this works will give you a good foundation in how sound is created with musical instruments, acoustic engineering, and technology.

PROPERTIES OF SOUND WAVES

Sound can be broken down into three required steps. First, an object must vibrate. When this happens, the object will make rapid back-and-forth movements. Next, those vibrations will move into a medium, a substance through which the vibration can travel. Examples of mediums include water, air, and wood. As the sound waves pass through a medium, they will travel in all directions. Finally, a receiver will pick up the sound. This receiver can be your ear, which will transform the sound wave into a signal immediately sent to the brain, which interprets the signal as a sound.

When it comes to the speed of sound, it's up to the medium. Sound takes roughly 5 seconds to travel 1 mile through the air at a temperature of 70° F (21° C). If the air warms, sound will travel even faster through it. Sound travels even faster through solid mediums like iron and stone and the liquid medium water.

The three basic properties of every sound wave are pitch, intensity, and quality. How low or high a sound is known as the *pitch*. Sounds made by faster vibrations cause higher pitches. The *intensity* of a sound is how quiet or loud it is. It is dependent on the intensity of the vibrations creating the sound. The *quality* of a sound refers to how pleasant or harsh it is. It is also referred to as timbre. These three properties describe all sounds, regardless of their origins or classifications.

MUSICAL INSTRUMENTS AND ACOUSTIC ENGINEERING

Musical instruments work differently depending on their classification. However, they all function on the same basic principle: Their noise is produced by vibrations. Acoustic engineers use this knowledge and how we hear things to design various technologies. Let's take a look at how this works.

How Musical Instruments Produce Sound

To produce sound, a musical instrument must vibrate at least partially and with enough intensity that the human ear can hear it. The four categories of musical instruments—woodwind, brass, percussion, and string—produce sound differently.

In the case of woodwind instruments, air must be blown across a reed attached to the instrument's mouthpiece. By doing this, you can vibrate the air through the instrument's tube, producing sound. These instruments typically have a note system in which you can cover various openings to produce different notes.

Brass instruments also require a mouthpiece, but the technique is slightly different. You will need to buzz your lips across that mouthpiece for these instruments. This action will produce the vibration through the instrument that creates the sound.

Percussion instruments are made from a hollow container with a material stretched tightly over the opening. Once the material is in place, a stick or hand strikes it to create a vibration and sound.

Changing the tightness of the material can alter the pitch of the sound.

You will need to pluck or bow the strings to create sound with a string instrument. This action creates vibrations that hit the instrument's hollow body. From there, the vibrations bounce off the instrument box, producing sound.

What is Acoustic Engineering?

Acoustic engineering is a specialty that focuses on sound and vibration. Engineers in this field typically focus their studies on designing, analyzing, and controlling sound. Examples of what these engineers do are finding ways to maximize the sound a guitar produces at a rock concert and minimizing background noise while recording a meeting.

Sounds are often created using amplifiers and speakers. The amplifier is a device that takes a signal delivered by another device, such as your laptop or cell phone, and generates a much larger copy of that signal. Once that copy is created, the amplifier transmits it to a speaker. The audio signal consists of electrical energy, which the speaker converts into mechanical sound waves that are detectable by your ears. The volume control determines how much of that sound gets released from the speakers.

Noise cancellation operates on a similar principle. Microphones pick up the unwanted low-frequency noise, neutralizing it before it can reach your ears. Noise-canceling headsets create a 180-degree phase-inverted sound to the unwanted sound. The result is a complete cancellation of both sounds.

Using this technology, acoustic engineers have developed methods of soundproofing to allow us to live more peaceful lives. These include soundproof materials that keep noise from traveling through walls in your home, at your school, and even at your parents' jobs.

One important factor all acoustic engineers consider is how your ears interpret sound. You see, your brain will interpret sound differently based on your situation. For example, if you're in a large group at a birthday party, you can still talk to your friend standing next to you because your brain is specifically focused on them. Likewise, you may interpret sounds and voices differently depending on other noises around you.

APPLICATIONS IN TECHNOLOGY

As we mentioned, one of the major technological advances in sound and acoustics has been noise-canceling headphones. They were originally developed to make flights more comfortable for pilots. Today, they're popular among consumers as they allow you to listen to your music or watch a video without the hassle of background noise.

High-resolution audio is another excellent technological application. While we've heard many different levels of quality when it comes to audio recordings, recent advancements have brought it to a new level. Today, you can buy devices that offer playback quality similar to the original recording.

Smart speakers are also an acoustic engineering marvel. They work by combining audio technology with artificial intelligence. Whether you favor Amazon Echo or Google Home, you'll get a high-quality device that responds quickly to your voice. You can easily control your audio content with a simple voice command.

While many great advances have already been made, more are in the works. You can expect things like 3D audio, virtual reality audio, and smart audio processing. With 3D audio, you'll have an experience like surround sound. It will be a truly immersive listening experience. Virtual reality audio will enhance the VR experience as it creates a more realistic soundscape in the VR world. Smart audio processing will introduce better noise cancelation and other enhancements easily adapted to your preferences.

Sound is truly amazing! Created by vibrations, it can travel great distances and be interpreted in many ways. With the improvements in technology, there are many great things to come in this field. Staying on the topic of things that move in waves, our next chapter will focus on light and optics.

CHAPTER FIFTEEN: LIGHT AND OPTICS

Light is the reason we can see. When it interacts with our eyes, it produces images that allow us to perceive what's in front of us. Over the centuries, scientists have harnessed that power to develop optical technologies that enhance our ability to see the tiniest objects or those that are lightyears away. Let's explore the behavior of light waves, different types of optical instruments, and applications in science and technology.

THE BEHAVIOR OF LIGHT WAVES

Light is a form of electromagnetic radiation with a unique property — it can be described as a stream of particles or a wave. In terms of light waves, light behaves in certain ways, including diffraction, refraction, and reflection.

Diffraction occurs when light waves come across an obstacle or enter through an opening. In either situation, the wave will bend around the object in question. If you've ever looked at the shiny side of a CD, you may have noticed patterns of light coming off the disc. This is diffraction. Another example of diffraction is the silver lining often seen in clouds. This occurs when light waves encounter the clouds and bend around them.

As light waves change the medium they travel through, they will change their direction of travel. This is a behavior typical of waves and is called refraction. It is very similar to how sound waves behave. As the light waves cross mediums, their speed also changes. A quick real-life example you can try right now is placing a straw in a glass of water. As you do this, you'll notice the straw seems to bend to the side after the point it is submerged. The light waves bend as they enter the water from the air, causing this distorted appearance.

Reflection is an important light wave behavior. The reflected light is the light we see. Additionally, how the light waves are reflected affects what colors we see. When a light wave travels through one medium and strikes another, some of that wave will bounce off the surface of the new medium. How reflective that surface is will determine how much of the wave is absorbed, transmitted, and reflected. The angle at which the light wave hits the new medium's surface is the same at which it will be reflected. There are two primary types of reflection: specular and diffuse. *Specular reflection* occurs when all light waves are reflected in the same direction, as with mirrors. When *diffuse reflection* occurs, light waves are reflected in multiple directions. This type of reflection occurs when the microscopic surface of the medium is rough.

OPTICAL INSTRUMENTS AND DEVICES

The most basic optical instrument is your eye. Light enters through the cornea and is immediately refracted. The section of the eye directly past the cornea is filled with a water-like solution. Your eyes' irises work like diaphragms, opening and closing the central hole that allows light to enter the eye. As they adjust the size of this opening, the amount of light allowed to enter will change. From there, the light waves are refracted through the various parts of the eye.

Light microscopes use light wave behaviors to allow the human eye to see microscopic objects and organisms that would otherwise be invisible. The light travels through the various lenses in the microscope, with each one magnifying the original image. One of the most commonly used microscopes is the compound microscope, which has at least two convex lenses.

Telescopes work similarly in that they produce enlarged images of objects, but the difference is that these objects only appear smaller because they're so far away. The two main types of telescopes are reflecting and refracting.

Another commonly used optical device is the camera. This device takes advantage of the behavior of light waves to create and store an image of an object. Depending on your camera type, this image may be stored on film or digitally. The process of forming the picture is the same, regardless of the storage method. Unlike microscopes and telescopes, a camera produces an image of reduced size from the original object.

APPLICATIONS IN SCIENCE AND TECHNOLOGY

Optics have many amazing applications in science and technology. One of the most significant applications has been in the healthcare industry with the invention of optical imaging. These advanced imaging techniques make it possible to precisely and visualize the human body. One example is optical coherence tomography (OCT). Ophthalmologists use it to diagnose and monitor many retinal diseases and conditions. OCT produces high-resolution, noninvasive images that allow the doctor to see the different layers of the eye easily. This allows for easy and early identification of diseases and enables the doctor to create a specialized treatment plan.

Microscopy techniques have also greatly advanced due to optical applications. Fluorescence microscopy has become refined enough to allow scientists to study biological specimens at the cellular and subcellular levels. Other advancements in microscopy have improved biomedical research and drug development. With this technology, scientists and researchers can see objects as small as a single molecule.

Optical technology has even improved the world of communication. High-speed data transmission can now be carried out over long distances because of fiber-optic communication systems, replacing traditional copper wires. This technology is the foundation for how the internet works. It allows for the rapid transfer of vast amounts of information worldwide. Photonic integrated circuits (PICs) are one advancement in optical technology that has improved communication. They integrate several optical components into a single chip, reducing power consumption and production costs and increasing data rates. Internet speed and bandwidth have dramatically increased with the advances in technology.

Another interesting technological application of optics is in autonomous vehicles. They use optical technology to perceive and navigate their surroundings accurately and safely. Light detection and ranging (LiDAR) systems create 3D maps using laser pulses to depict the surrounding environment. This system allows the vehicle to recognize and avoid obstacles, other vehicles, and pedestrians.

Additionally, an autonomous (self-driving) vehicle's perception system depends largely on optical sensors and cameras. These features allow the vehicle to recognize important things, including road signs, pedestrians, and lane markings, making travel much safer.

If you've ever used virtual reality or augmented reality, you've experienced optical technology in action. Head-mounted displays would not effectively immerse users into a virtual world without optics, which produce high-resolution images.

Because light has such interesting behaviors, science and technology can use it for many different applications. The future of optical technology is nearly limitless with the advances that can be made. In our next chapter together, we'll explore the fascinating world of geological processes.

CHAPTER SIXTEEN: GEOLOGICAL PROCESSES

Earth is full of mysteries. Geological processes, while truly powerful and capable of producing amazing formations, can be quite destructive. From volcanoes to earthquakes, the raw power behind these processes can destroy everything for miles. Most of these processes rely on plate tectonics. What's more, these processes leave evidence behind that allows us to interpret geological time. So, let's get into how geological processes work to take the mystery out of these powerful events.

VOLCANOES AND EARTHQUAKES

Volcanoes and earthquakes are similar because they both involve movement deep within Earth. Depending on the severity of the activity, they can cause significant physical vibrations and damage. The mechanism behind the activity of volcanoes and earthquakes is often the same—tectonic plate movement under Earth's crust.

How Volcanoes Work

Volcanoes are openings in Earth's crust that may be active or inactive. When an active volcano erupts, melted rock and hot gases reach the surface. Once on the surface, the melted rock or magma is called lava. The lava will either exit the ground slowly through a crack or fissure or explode violently into the air. Because of the potential for a powerful explosion, volcanoes can be deadly and cause significant damage. It is estimated that there are currently 1,500 volcanoes worldwide that could be potentially active.

When lava is released from a volcano, its temperature ranges from 1,300 to 2,200 °F (700 to 1,200 °C). Initially, it glows a bright, hot red. However, as it cools, it turns into a rock. If a volcanic eruption is especially powerful, it can send bits of lava far into the air. This lava will cool into tiny pieces of rock, known as volcanic dust or ash. Volcanic dust can travel by wind for thousands of miles, while volcanic ash can coat everything for miles surrounding the volcano.

In addition to the expulsion of the lava, poisonous gases may be released. They may be combined with volcanic ash or other debris. The combination travels in a fiery cloud known as a pyroclastic flow.

Earth's crust consists of tectonic plates. These plates move slowly along the crust and sometimes overlap—most of the world's volcanoes are along the boundaries between these plates. It's very common for violent eruptions to take place in locations where these plates cross over one another. When one plate's edge is forced under the edge of another, magma rises to the surface. These volcanoes are so explosive because of all the hot gases mixed in with the magma. Most violently erupting volcanoes can be found in the Pacific Ocean's Ring of Fire.

A volcano may also form in areas where two plates separate from one another. As the plates separate, magma rises between them, escaping through fissures in the ground. These volcanoes commonly form along the Mid-Atlantic Ridge, a mountain range found under the Atlantic Ocean. Iceland was formed by the volcanoes in the range's northern section.

In some places on Earth's crust, volcanoes form from hot spots. These volcanoes do not exist on plate boundaries. Instead, they are locations where molten rock rises to the surface from deep below the crust. An example of hot-spot volcanoes is those found in Hawaii.

Volcanic eruptions can also create new landforms, which are also called volcanoes. The two most common land formations are stratovolcanoes and shield volcanoes. A stratovolcano is a cone-shaped mountain formed by thousands of eruptions over millions of years. These eruptions produced hardened layers of lava and ash that eventually formed a massive mountain. Japan's Mount Fuji is one of the most well-known stratovolcanoes.

Shield volcanoes are dome-shaped and less steep than stratovolcanoes. However, they can be massive. Some shield volcanoes located under the sea erupt and grow into islands. Hawaii's volcanoes are classified as shield volcanoes.

How Earthquakes Happen

Believe it or not, earthquakes happen millions of times each year! However, most are so small that they cannot be felt. The most powerful can cause extreme destruction, including landslides, flooding, and more. The most damage and deaths often occur in heavily populated areas, as there are more buildings to collapse, windows to break, and fires to start.

Like volcanoes, earthquakes are the result of tectonic plate movements. Instead of being connected, tectonic plates are located very close together. The area along their edges where they meet is called a fault. The heat in Earth's core can cause currents throughout the crust, which cause the tectonic plates to bump, scrape, and drag along one another. The result is an earthquake.

Every earthquake has an epicenter. This spot on the surface correlates to the underground location where the tectonic plates interacted. Seismic waves are ripples that travel from the epicenter and can cause people to feel vibrations many miles from the earthquake's origin. Just how far away you can feel an earthquake depends on its magnitude. The magnitude is measured based on the duration and strength of the seismic waves. The higher the number, the greater the power of the earthquake.

Once the crust settles following an earthquake, it's common for aftershocks to occur. Aftershocks are typically less powerful than the original earthquake but can still pack a powerful punch. Currently, scientists cannot predict when an earthquake will happen, but researchers are putting a lot of effort into demystifying the science.

PLATE TECTONICS AND GEOLOGICAL FORMATIONS

We've already discussed some of what plate tectonics are, but understanding how our planet is structured is important to understand this theory. Geological formations can also result from the activity of tectonic plates. We'll also dive into the different types of formations and how they are produced.

What Are Plate Tectonics?

Plate tectonics is a theory that states Earth's crust is made up of large, mobile plates. Everything on the planet rests on these plates of solid rock. Beneath the plates is a partially melted layer of rock that they constantly move over.

As these plates move, they interact with those they have boundaries with. Depending on their positioning, these interactions will vary. In one scenario, the plates will simply slide alongside one another. In another, two plates may crash into each other, resulting in one sliding over the edge of the other, destroying it, or the two rising to create a mountainous structure. In the final type of interaction, two plates may move apart.

While these plates have been moving for millions of years, they've also caused the movement of continents. Plate tectonics cause continental drift, which is the slow movement of continents across the planet's surface. Scientists believe it will take approximately 500 million years for the continents to move together to form one supercontinent and separate once more.

The most recent supercontinent was Pangea. It formed approximately 270 million years ago along a tectonic plate boundary. Eventually, the continent broke apart on this boundary, and magma rose to fill the space in the middle, which became the Atlantic Ocean floor. Initially, Pangea broke into two supercontinents that spread across the planet, only to break apart into the continental structure we have today. Scientists project that Earth will have another supercontinent in about 250 million years.

How Geological Formations Are Created

The process of geological formation can be simply defined as the method of rock production. Igneous, metamorphic, and sedimentary rocks are each produced differently. *Igneous rocks* result from the cooling and hardening of magma. *Metamorphic rocks* are created when already formed rocks are transformed through heat or pressure. *Sedimentary rocks* result from the layering and cementing of smaller pieces of rock over time.

Tectonic activity can have a lot to do with geological formations. Igneous rock forms when the plates move and release magma, causing volcanic activity. Additionally, the movement of the plates can create faults, folds, and mesas, among other geological formations.

Mountains are an example of a geological formation created by tectonic plates. They are formed when two plates crash into one another. Instead of sinking below the other, the plates will crumple up, folding until the rocks are forced into a mountain range. With the continual collision of the plates, the mountains will grow taller. The Rocky Mountain range is one such example.

Sometimes, when two plates move apart, they create a rift valley. This type of valley is a stretched-out trough formed in Earth's crust. As the plates separate, large-scale faulting of the crust occurs, resulting in a reduction in the land between the faults, which creates a rift valley. Volcanoes, island arcs, and deep ocean trenches are other geological formations produced by tectonic activity.

GEOLOGICAL TIME SCALES

Geologists can determine specific timelines based on geological time scales. The geological rock record is based on geological events, including mountain building and erosion. As we mentioned, over many millions of years, the continents have traveled slowly across the planet. In addition, the oceans and mountain ranges have moved with them. What was a vast ocean millions of years ago may be a desert land today.

The first geological time scales evaluated the order of rocks in a sedimentary rock sequence. In this sequence, the topmost layer was the youngest rock, and the bottommost layer was the oldest. Scientists found a more powerful geological time tool in fossils. In 1859, the *Origin of Species* by Charles Darwin was published. His work led other geologists to determine that specific fossils were only found in certain rock layers. This knowledge resulted in the first generalized geological time scale.

Geologic time is divided into several distinct eons. *Precambrian* time represents all events from when Earth's crust formed to the beginning of the Phanerozoic eon, roughly 542 million years ago. This period accounts for more than 80% of Earth's history. Precambrian time is divided into two eons: the Archaean and the Proterozoic.

Our current geological period is the *Phanerozoic* eon, which started roughly 542 million years ago. It includes the Paleozoic, the Mesozoic, and the Cenozoic eras. The *Paleozoic* era was approximately 291 million years long. At the start of this era, plants and animals were aquatic, living in the ocean, and the climate was mild. By its end, half of all animal groups and most plants evolved.

Next came the *Mesozoic* era, which lasted approximately 185.5 million years. This era is frequently called the Age of the Reptiles because reptiles were the dominant animal life form. The dinosaurs appeared in the earliest period of this era, but they completely disappeared by the end of its third and final era.

Finally, the *Cenozoic* era began 65.5 million years ago and continues today. This era could be considered an age of mammals because of the development and spread of early mammal species. In addition, this era saw the coming and going of the ice ages. This massive ice movement formed the Great Lakes, the Alps, the Himalayas, and the Grand Canyon.

If you've ever experienced an earthquake or observed an erupting volcano, you've witnessed firsthand how powerful geological processes can be. It's amazing to think that, beneath our feet, tectonic plates are constantly in motion, and the continents we live on aren't stationary. With this newfound knowledge of geological processes, you've learned about the driving force of tectonic plates. Let's leave the world of geological sciences behind and switch gears for our next chapter. If you're interested in sports, you'll love learning about sports and athletic equipment.

CHAPTER SEVENTEEN: SPORTS AND ATHLETIC EQUIPMENT

The last things you probably associate sports and athletics with are science and technology. However, we wouldn't have the things we have today without the major advancements in both fields. From the physics behind your favorite sports to the innovative design of your equipment, let's dive into the fascinating world of how sports work.

PHYSICS OF SPORTS

Physics is the science of matter, focusing on important aspects such as movement through space and time. As such, it is central to how sports work.

For example, work and energy are two important elements studied in physics. Work refers to the result of a force acting on an object to move it a specific distance. Because of this, work and force are proportional, which means they are balanced. Additionally, work and energy are closely tied together. Work moves energy from one spot to another.

So, what does this mean for an athlete? Let's look at pole vaulting for a minute. What begins as chemical energy is transformed into kinetic energy as the vaulter starts running. As the pole deforms, part of the energy converts into potential energy. The remaining energy converts into gravitational potential energy. That energy then reverts to kinetic energy once the vaulter falls from the bar.

In figure skating, athletes often rely on angular momentum, which measures how much rotational motion an object has. When there are no external factors affecting the skater, their angular momentum will be conserved, remaining nearly constant. As they draw in one of their legs and both arms, they reduce their axis of rotation and some of their mass, reducing friction with the air. As a result, angular momentum is conserved, and rotational velocity must increase to make up the difference.

Friction is a force resulting from the resistance of one surface being displaced over another and elements of materials sliding against one another. No matter the sport, friction is a force that must be overcome. It's a key driving force in the success of ice skating. The friction caused by the skater's movements slightly melts the ice, creating a very thin layer of water between the ice and the skate. This allows the skater to essentially glide across the ice.

Special coatings are used in cycling to help reduce air resistance or friction caused by contact with the air. In sports like baseball, the smoothness of the ball determines how well it will travel through the air, resisting the frictional pull of the air.

TECHNOLOGY IN ATHLETIC PERFORMANCE

There's no doubt about it: Technology has advanced beyond belief in the sports world. Today, you can find all wearables that allow you to monitor important aspects of your training and health. Smartwatches count your steps, monitor your heart rate, and track your workout route.

Heart rate monitors allow for a real-time view of how intense your workout is. Everyone has a target heart rate they're supposed to achieve during high-intensity workouts. These wearable devices allow athletes to ensure they're putting in all the effort they need to achieve their fitness goals.

GPS trackers are great for running and cycling. They monitor where you've gone, your pace, and how far you've traveled. If you're into endurance training, this type of wearable is something you'd want to have on you for every workout session.

Many athletes also use wearables to track their rest and recovery periods. Getting enough sleep is super important for everyone, especially when you work hard on your fitness goals. When you don't get enough sleep, your body will not properly recover from the physical stress exercise places on it. Using a wearable device that monitors sleep, and recovery can help ensure you restore your energy.

Another popular technological innovation is video analysis tools. Many athletes perfect their form by watching videos of their performances. Along with their coaches and trainers, they review the video footage to note areas that need correction and improvement. These review sessions allow for dramatic improvement in their overall athletic performance.

Modern athletics are driven by data when it comes to making decisions. All these tools allow athletes to analyze the data collected to make better decisions about their training and recovery. They can identify their specific strengths and weaknesses, customize training programs, and work toward preventing injuries.

There are many great examples of technology in action in modern sports. For instance, in the NBA, players use tracking technology to optimize their strategy and performance. Similarly, swimmers use wearables to help keep track of strokes and efficiency during turns.

EQUIPMENT DESIGN
AND INNOVATION

Some sports equipment is specially designed to help protect athletes from injury and easily communicate with team members. A great example is helmets. Today, many American football helmets are equipped with radio or video capabilities to allow those on the field to communicate easily with support staff. In addition, these helmets are made with multiple layers to keep players safe from head injuries during impacts.

Another impact-oriented piece of equipment is the mouthguard. In many sports, contact can occur between players or even with the ball. These impacts can be severely damaging without protective gear. Mouthguards are typically worn on the upper teeth and can be custom-fitted by a dentist for the best protection.

Footwear is also specifically designed to aid players in various sports. Cleats help provide traction on potentially slippery grass, ensuring players always keep their footing. This helps them keep a fast pace and prevents slip-and-fall accidents.

In other areas, lightweight and flexible equipment, including sports clothing, is the key to being the most successful athlete. These sports include cycling, boxing, and dance. Having the greatest range of movement is essential to mobility, reducing drag, and enhancing muscle support. Options include microfiber, Spandex, and Lycra.

Surfing has also seen its fair share of innovation. More advanced boards have been developed that are lighter and more buoyant. This material advancement ensures that surfers have the best wave-riding capabilities.

Your favorite sports are jam-packed with science, from gliding over the ice to soaring through the air while pole vaulting. With this look at how it all works, you now have a different way of seeing things like swimming and skating. While you've learned a bit about injury prevention with specialized sports equipment, our next chapter will focus on how medical imaging and diagnostic tools work.

CHAPTER EIGHTEEN:
MEDICAL IMAGING
AND DIAGNOSTIC TOOLS

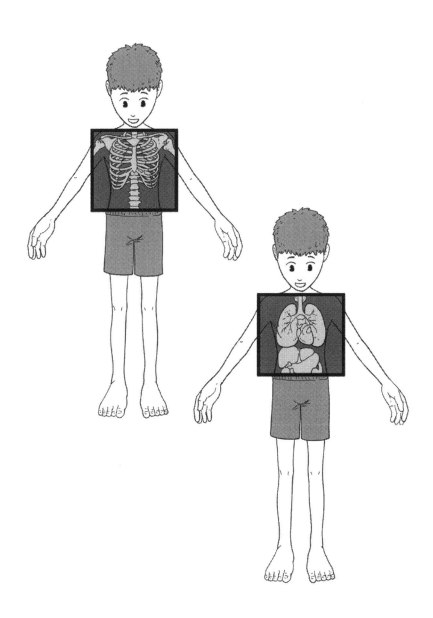

Medicine's success depends on a doctor's ability to diagnose the condition accurately. To do this, they use medical imaging and diagnostic tools. Understanding how these techniques and tools work will allow us to learn how doctors do part of their important jobs.

IMAGING TECHNIQUES
(X-RAYS, MRI, CT)

If you've ever broken a bone or had a major sickness, you might have had special imaging done at the hospital. The techniques often used are X-rays, MRI, and CT scans. Each is unique and used for different purposes, but all three provide images of something inside your body.

The *X-ray* is one of the most basic imaging techniques doctors use today. It creates an image like a photograph of your insides. In the final product, your bones look white, and anything squishy inside you, like your muscles, will look gray. Any air will appear black.

X-rays help doctors and dentists find the source of pain and other problems inside your body. They use the information from the X-rays to help determine the best treatment options to help you feel your best. You may also need an X-ray one more time after treatment to make sure everything goes as planned.

A *CT scan* offers a more detailed image of things going on inside your body. Doctors use this technique when an X-ray doesn't provide enough detail of the problem. The device has a lot of moving parts and a big tunnel in the middle. When you have a CT scan done, you'll lay on a bed that moves through this tunnel while images are taken of various parts of your body.

Sometimes, to get the best picture, the technician taking the scan will give you a dye called contrast. This is used to make your images clear, allowing the doctors to see exactly what's wrong. The most important part about having a CT scan done is staying still through the whole process, which could be just a few minutes to a half hour. If the technician thinks you'll need help staying still, they may give you a medication called a sedative to help keep you calm and still.

An MRI machine is very similar in appearance to a CT scanner with a large tunnel. However, they work differently. The *MRI* uses a magnetic field that works with a computer to capture images of your body. MRIs are used to look at your internal tissues, like your organs and muscles. Like with a CT scan, you may need a contrast to make the pictures clearer. This machine is very loud while it works, so the technician may give you headphones or earplugs, so you don't have to hear it.

When all three types of images are collected, they must be viewed by a special doctor called a radiologist. While these images may not look important to you, this doctor will know exactly what to look for to determine how to treat you.

LABORATORY DIAGNOSTICS

In addition to medical imaging, doctors also use laboratory diagnostics to assess common health problems, ranging from blood testing to taking urine samples.

If you have an illness, your doctor may want to run blood tests to see if they can identify what's wrong. A commonly used test is the complete blood count or CBC. This test checks the different levels of all your blood cells, including red cells, white cells, and platelets. The doctor will use the information from the test to check for problems like anemia and infections.

A more prevalent disease that many people face today is diabetes. Because of this, doctors frequently check blood glucose levels. Glucose is the sugar located in your blood. The doctor will use the levels reported in the bloodwork to determine if the patient has diabetes and how best to manage it.

Urine tests are commonly used to detect urinary tract infections. Additionally, they're one of the first options doctors use to check for pregnancy in expectant mothers. These tests are typically called urinalysis.

Other diagnostics fall under microbiological testing, which means they check for bacteria or parasites. One common test is the strep throat swab. This test uses a large cotton swab to take a sample from the back of someone's throat to see if they have a strep infection, a common cause of sore throats.

Biochemical diagnostic tests assess the levels of enzymes, proteins, and essential minerals in the body. The liver is examined using liver function tests that evaluate the number of enzymes and proteins in the blood.

Genetic testing has come a long way and is more frequently used today than before. DNA sequencing is a great example of this type of diagnostic testing. It analyzes genetic material to identify whether someone has inherited specific conditions or is at risk for others.

Another type of genetic testing that has taken off is newborn screening. More than ever, parents want to know the whole story behind the health of their newborn children. These tests can reveal whether the baby has metabolic, endocrine, or genetic disorders.

ADVANCES IN MEDICAL TECHNOLOGY

We've seen tremendous advances in medical technology that have led to improvements in diagnostics and overall healthcare. One of these advances has been in the realm of mRNA technology. *Messenger RNA* (mRNA) is single-stranded RNA required for protein synthesis. This technology uses synthetic RNA to direct cells to produce specific protein molecules. It has been extremely important in creating certain vaccinations, including those for COVID-19.

In addition, mRNA technology can be used to detect various illnesses early. It offers a more precise diagnosis that alternative methods don't. Patient outcomes are significantly improved because of the ability to more accurately and efficiently diagnose illnesses and diseases. The likelihood of false outcomes is significantly reduced with this diagnostic technology.

CRISPR (clustered regularly interspaced short palindromic repeats) is a specialized gene-editing tool. Scientists can use CRISPR technology to delete or modify specific genes within an organism's DNA. CRISPR-based testing also accurately diagnoses genetic mutations associated with many diseases and conditions.

With genetic testing, doctors can better determine if an individual is at risk for certain diseases based on their specific genetic makeup. Individuals are granted personalized treatment based on their specific genomic profiles.

Artificial intelligence and data integration are two more major advances in medical technology that aid in diagnostics. Data integration consolidates and analyzes data from various sources, including lab tests and electronic health records. Integrating all the data doctors can access is important for making the most accurate diagnosis for every patient.

AI uses algorithms to analyze large volumes of data, detect patterns, and identify abnormalities the human eye might overlook without assistance. Tools with AI assistance can help with the interpretation of medical images. In addition, by analyzing patient data, these AI algorithms can help predict disease progression and create personalized treatment options.

Nanomedicine relies on nanotechnology, which uses materials and devices on the nanoscale to monitor, diagnose, and treat illnesses. These nanoscale tools can target specific tissues or cells affected by the disease, enabling the best treatment possible. Specially coated nanoparticles are frequently used to enhance medical imaging. For example, gold-coated nanoparticles are tools used in cancer detection, as the special particles will accumulate at the tumor site, making it easier for medical imaging devices to recognize them.

Medical 3D printing enables medical professionals to craft patient-specific medical devices, models, and implants. Surgeons can use 3D printing to create replicas of the patient's anatomy to perfect their strategy for the upcoming operation. Researchers are currently investigating the possibility of using 3D printing to engineer tissues. If successful, this would allow for the creation of fully functional organs ready for transplant. Bioprinting techniques are being developed that could lead to personalized medicine by creating organs and tissues from the patient's cells. This would result in a major decrease in organ rejection during transplant surgeries.

As you can see, the tools used in modern medicine are truly amazing. They allow doctors to see what's happening inside you to provide the best possible treatment for an illness or medical condition. Similar to the advancements in the medical field, robotics has made leaps and bounds over the years. Today, robotics and artificial intelligence are important parts of many industries. Our final chapter together will cover how these parts work.

CHAPTER NINETEEN:
ROBOTICS AND ARTIFICIAL
INTELLIGENCE

Chances are you've seen a movie or TV show with robots, but have you ever thought about how they work? Robotics and artificial intelligence are cornerstones of technological advancements across many industries today. Let's dive into how they work and what you can use them for.

PRINCIPLES OF ROBOTICS

Several important principles govern how robots are designed, developed, and operated. These principles are important for many things, including helping researchers maintain ethical practices.

The first important principle is the concept of autonomy. Robots should be able to act independently without human intervention. This is made possible by specialized programming that equips the robots with algorithms and sensors that let them make their own decisions and perform their own actions. Autonomy is an important feature of robots because it allows them to perform jobs independent of human interaction. Robots take on many of the jobs that are unsafe for humans.

Those sensors that aid in autonomy are also important because they gather data from the environment to provide information to the robot. They enable the robot to understand its surroundings to freely navigate and interact with its environment. This means the robot can walk around obstacles, pick up objects, and perform tasks as needed.

Robots must also have effective control systems to make sure the robot's actions are precise and accurate. These control systems have different parts, including algorithms, feedback loops, and real-time processing. In addition, they must have effective, user-friendly interfaces that allow for easy human-robot interaction.

Robots have three main parts: the sensors, the controller, and the actuator. *Sensors*, as mentioned, provide environmental information that allows the robot to respond appropriately. The *controller* controls the robot's movements through a feedback control system operated by a computer program. The *actuators* provide the physical movement through parts like pistons and motors.

While robots can take on jobs that many humans dislike or pose a safety risk to humans, they must also be properly programmed to ensure the safety of the humans working around them. Robotic programming must account for the potential for accidents and enable safety protocols. This will protect anyone who works besides, with, or on these devices.

AI & MACHINE LEARNING

Another important feature of robotics is its use of artificial intelligence and machine learning. Through these tools, robots can improve their performance and learn from experience. The goal of machine learning is to enable AI to enhance its accuracy step by step by imitating how humans learn.

Machine learning has three parts. It starts with a decision process. Data is input into a machine learning algorithm, which makes a prediction or classification. The algorithm will estimate any patterns identified within the input data.

The models also have an error function used to evaluate the model's predictions. When supplied with known examples, the error function can make comparisons assessing the model's accuracy.

The third part of machine learning is a model optimization process. When the model is compared to the known example, weights will be adjusted if it is found that the model can fit better with the training set's data points. The algorithm will repeat the process of evaluating and optimizing until it meets the desired level of accuracy.

Machine learning can be supervised, unsupervised, or semi-supervised. Supervised machine learning relies on labeled datasets. These datasets are input into the algorithms and used to classify or predict outcomes accurately. This type of learning is geared toward solving many real-world problems, such as identifying and moving spam to its own folder in your email.

Unsupervised machine learning analyzes unlabeled datasets. The process finds hidden patterns within the data and requires no human intervention to do its job. Unsupervised machine learning optimizes exploratory data analysis and image and pattern recognition.

Semi-supervised machine learning is the ideal combination of supervised and unsupervised aspects. Extracting information from a larger, unlabeled dataset takes a smaller set of labeled data. This type of machine learning is the best solution for cases when there is not enough labeled data for supervised machine learning.

IMPACT ON INDUSTRY & EVERYDAY LIFE

Robotics and machine learning can profoundly impact industry and everyday life. They can make average tasks easier and keep humans safer.

Advancements have been made in the automotive industry, with autonomous cars becoming more mainstream. However, with these advances come important questions. While these cars are less likely to have an accident than manned vehicles, they're not infallible. So, should they have an accident, the question is, who should be held liable?

Other concerns have also become more prevalent with the rise of AI in the workforce. Many fear that machines will completely replace humans in many industries. However, as with most technological advances, AI will likely shift the focus of the job market, aligning the demand for jobs with other needs.

Robotics and machine learning can also improve how we live. They can improve our online experiences by custom-tailoring our browsing experiences to fit our preferences and needs.

In various industries, humans and robots can work safely together to accomplish important tasks more quickly and efficiently. Because of the easy-to-use interfaces, humans and robots can easily interact to share information and collaborate effectively.

Implementing robotics in industrial settings can help reduce costs and human error, making companies more profitable and producing goods faster. Automation can allow for improved efficiency and consistency.

Robotics and machine learning are becoming central elements in industrial settings. They enable workers to complete complex tasks safely and efficiently. In addition, they're becoming more common in many everyday places, including driverless cars. One thing is for sure: The sky's the limit when it comes to the advances we'll see in the coming years.

CONCLUSION

Now that you've looked at a bit of how everything works, you have a ton of new knowledge to share with your friends and family. You can take what you've learned here and look at everything in your life with a new perspective, from playing baseball to cooking dinner.

REFLECTION ON THE JOURNEY OF DISCOVERY

We've traveled a long distance through space, athletics, cooking, and so much more. Throughout our journey, we've learned that curiosity is essential to understanding how things work. The more you explore, the greater your thirst for knowledge will become.

Gaining knowledge and understanding of the mysteries behind how stuff works can offer you a completely different perspective on the things you love the most. For example, knowing how you glide across the ice in your skates makes the process seem more magical.

THE ONGOING EVOLUTION OF UNDERSTANDING

Science and technology are always changing and improving. What we knew ten years ago is nothing compared to today. Because of this, it's important to continually improve our understanding of how things work.

As things evolve and advance, so, too, must our knowledge. There is always something new and exciting to learn. With every new technological advancement, you can expand your perspective and enhance your understanding.

ENCOURAGEMENT OF CURIOSITY & EXPLORATION

As we conclude our journey into the wonderful world of how stuff works, don't let this be the end of your curiosity. Keep exploring and learning new things. Your curiosity is like your secret, hidden superpower.

There are secrets to uncover all around you, from the simplest kitchen gadgets to the most complex video gaming systems. Never stop asking questions or looking for the answers to how everything works.

This book should be just the beginning—there's a never-ending world of information to obtain. Grab your thinking cap and fire up your imagination as you continue your adventure. The joy of discovery never ends so long as you stay curious.

Made in United States
Orlando, FL
08 December 2024

55180846R00080